MODERN PRODUCTION MANAGEMENT: A JAPANESE EXPERIENCE

ASIAN PRODUCTIVITY ORGANIZATION
TOKYO

MODERN PRODUCTION MANAGEMENT: A JAPANESE EXPERIENCE

by

Eiji Ogawa

Professor, Department of Economics
Nagoya University

1984
ASIAN PRODUCTIVITY ORGANIZATION
TOKYO

Some other titles published by the ASIAN PRODUCTIVITY ORGANIZATION:

- Bases for Science and Technology Promotion in Developing Countries
- Guide to Quality Control, (Second Revised Edition)
- Japan's Quality Control Circles, (Third Reprint)
- Technoeconomics – Concepts and Cases
- Japanese-style Management: Its Foundations and Prospects
- Organizing for Higher Productivity: An Analysis of Japanese Systems and Practices
- Profitability Analysis for Managerial and Engineering Decisions
- Management by Objectives: A Japanese Experience
- How to Measure Maintenance Performance
- Measuring and Enhancing the Productivity of Service and Government Organizations, (Third Reprint)
- Preparing for Standardization, Certification & Quality Control
- Productivity Through Consultancy in Small Industrial Enterprises
- Guidelines for Management Consultants in Asia
- 100 Management Charts
- Preparing Feasibility Studies in Asia

Designed and Printed in Hong Kong by
NORDICA INTERNATIONAL LIMITED
for
ASIAN PRODUCTIVITY ORGANIZATION
4-14, Akasaka 8-chome
Minato-ku, Tokyo 107, Japan

ISBN 92-833-1071-3 (Casebound)
92-833-1072-1 (Limpbound)

FOREWORD

This book interprets modern production management as a means of controlling the input-output sequence as a dynamic relationship. The impact of huge and complicated production systems, severe competition in the market, and the continuous advancement in science and technology are taken into consideration. Production management is not a monopoly of large corporations. It should be used by smaller firms in a simplified format to minimize input and maximize output in order to reach operational goals in the face of severe competition.

The author compares complex systems with relatively simple systems. Production management itself is not cost free. Production management is meaningless unless it is cost efficient. One should not overlook this point in its discussion.

The book is divided into two parts: Part One comprises five chapters. Chapter 1 deals with the historical evolution of production management. Chapter 2 delineates different types of production management applicable to different manufacturing formats. Evolution of the manufacturing format is also discussed in this chapter. Chapters 3 and 4 explore technical and organizational changes and their impact on production management. Chapter 5 views production management in connection with corporate organization and strategy to complete Part One.

In Part Two, Chapter 6 discusses the relationship between market and production management. Chapters 7, 8 and 9 discuss work standardization, production planning, and scheduling and inventory control, respectively. In order to realize maximum efficiency in fulfilling corporate objectives, it is desirable to establish an integrated management plan which covers such parameters as quality, labour, time, quantity, cost, profit, strategies for new business, and environmental changes. The Toyota production system does exactly that. As a successful example of integrated production management, Chapter 10 describes production management at Toyota Motors.

Effective production management seeks balance between entrepreneurship and worker motivation. This will remain unchanged despite automation, because fully automated plants cannot be created and operated without people. Plant design, construction, testing, supervision, and maintenance are all done by people. True production management, as emphasized in this book, is human-oriented and is accomplished by persuasive, effective motivation programmes.

This book summarizes my views on such production management and I hope that it will give some insights to readers. I also want to express my appreciation of the Asian Productivity Organization for publishing this English version of "Modern Production Management." I am also thankful to Dr. James L. Riggs, Head, Industrial Engineering Department of the Oregon State University for going through the manuscript and offering concrete suggestions to improve the English text.

Eiji Ogawa

Tokyo, September, 1984

TABLE OF CONTENTS

FOREWORD i

PART ONE:
BASIS OF PRODUCTION MANAGEMENT

Chapter 1 PRODUCTION MANAGEMENT 1
1.1 What is Production Management? 1
1.2 History of Production Management 4
1.3 Production Management Today – A Systems Viewpoint 6
1.4 Production Management Today – Two Types of Control 9
1.5 Production Management Today – Productivity Improvement 10

Chapter 2 PRODUCTION FORMAT AND MANAGEMENT . . . 13
2.1 Classification of Production Formats 13
2.2 Characteristics of Production Formats 16
2.3 Production Format and Its Management 17
2.4 Production Formats for Small and Medium-sized Firms 19

Chapter 3 PRODUCTION MANAGEMENT, AUTOMATION AND COMPUTERIZATION 23
3.1 From Manual to Machine Processing 23
3.2 Automation and Production Management . . . 25
3.3 Computerization and Production Management 26
3.4 Economic Efficiency of Automation and Computerization 29

3.5 Automation and Computerization by Small and Medium-sized Firms 31

Chapter 4 PRODUCTION MANAGEMENT AND THE WORKER 33

4.1 Changing Demography 33

4.2 Change in the Role of Workers 35

4.3 Production Management and the Socio-technical Approach 36

4.4 Pre-production Arrangements and Production Management 39

4.5 Workers in Small and Medium-sized Firms . . . 41

Chapter 5 STRATEGY, ORGANIZATION, AND PRODUCTION MANAGEMENT 43

5.1 Strategies and the Production Process 43

5.2 Production Strategy and Management 45

5.3 Production Organization and Management . . . 48

5.4 Strategies and Organizations for Smaller Corporations 53

PART TWO: DEPLOYMENT OF PRODUCTION MANAGEMENTT

Chapter 6 DEMAND FLUCTUATION AND PRODUCTION MANAGEMENT 59

6.1 Changing Needs 59

6.2 Cost Reduction-oriented Production Management 61

6.3 Small Scale Production of Large Variety of Product 63

6.4 Shorter Lead-Time and On-Time Delivery . . . 66

6.5 High Quality and Low Production Cost 68

6.6 Smaller Firms in Unstable Markets 71

Chapter 7 WORK STANDARDIZATION 73

7.1 Standard: Meaning and Conditions 73

7.2 Formulation of Work Standards – Traditional Method 74

7.3 Time Synthesizing Analysis and Multi-Unit Supervision 77

7.4 Learning Effect 79

7.5 Work Standardization in Small and Medium-Sized Firms 81

Chapter 8 PRODUCTION PLANNING 83

8.1 What is Production Planning? 83

8.2 Production Planning Methodologies 86

8.3 Simulation Modeling 90

8.4 Estimation of Sales 91

8.5 Production Planning for Smaller Firms 93

Chapter 9 SCHEDULING AND INVENTORY CONTROL 95

9.1 Introduction 95

9.2 Materials Requirements Planning 97

9.3 Scheduling Control 98

9.4 Inventory Control 102

9.5 Scheduling and Inventory Control for Smaller Firms 104

Chapter 10 INTEGRATED PRODUCTION MANAGEMENT ... 107

10.1 Integrated Production Management and Toyota-style Production Management 107

10.2 The "Kan-Ban" System 109

10.3 Elimination of Waste 112

10.4 Inventory Compression 114

10.5 Application to Smaller Firms 116

APPENDIX: SIGNIFICANCE OF TOYOTA PRODUCTION SYSTEM IN MODERN PRODUCTION MANAGEMENT 119

PART ONE

BASIS OF PRODUCTION MANAGEMENT

Chapter 1
PRODUCTION MANAGEMENT

The methodology of production management is subject to drastic changes in the midst of technological innovations. This chapter deals with the historical evolution of production management methodology in order to give a new definition to that concept, and to clarify that production management is based on system concepts. The last part of the chapter discusses two types of control, characteristic of modern production management and their application for productivity improvement.

1.1 WHAT IS PRODUCTION MANAGEMENT?

What does "production management" mean? First, "production" means to make goods. Therefore, production management should mean the management of goods making. What then, does the word "management" mean specifically?

1.1.1 Management

It is difficult to define the word "management" in a way that covers all ramifications of its meaning. In this book, "management" is used in a broad sense not limited to the exercise of control. This can be illustrated in schedule management as an example. Smooth job execution is impossible without proper scheduling. Normally, schedules are formulated and implemented according to a set of predetermined procedures. However, in order to keep up with a rapidly changing world, such pre-determined procedures should change from time to time. In other words, schedule management can no longer remain static. Corporations must work out optimal ways of formulating and executing schedules in accordance with the changing environment. Rather than sticking to one set of predetermined procedures all the time, corporations should look for procedures that will better facilitate the realization of corporate objectives.

Coming back to "production management", the word "management" is generally considered to consist of 1) planning, 2) implementation, and

3) control. This management "cycle" is not a monolithic concept, but one realized in a variety of ways depending on different types and aspects of production.

1.1.2 How to Manage Production

What are the specific features of production? Consider the management of shop floor work in a manufacturing plant complete with building, equipment, and tools. Here, the planning phase should cover work steps and their improvement. Then, the plan is carried out in the implementation phase, followed by the controlling phase, with the progress made in achieving the planned target being the main concern.

Next, consider a plant construction project, including the procurement and installation of plant, equipment, and tools. This is a type of production that probably only takes place once in half a decade or so for a manufacturing firm. How is such production managed? The planning phase starts with a corporate decision on capital investment. A detailed construction project encompasses various planning activities. When construction work begins in accordance with the decisions made at the planning phase, the project enters the implementation phase. In the course of implementation, the control measures taken to see that daily schedules, quality, and costs are adhered to become the controlling phase.

As discussed above, there are two types of production processes, one making goods using equipment and the other making the equipment or the production system itself. In the case of the manufacturing industry, the former process may be called "production" and the latter, "the preparation for production". In the face of prevalent rapid economic change and technological advancement, production can never remain static. With robots being introduced into production plants and factories being built based on revolutionary design concepts, both the "making of goods" and "preparation for production" through changes in production equipment are taking place. Production no longer limited to making goods epitomizes the two dimensional nature of the production process.

Production management may be defined as the planning, implementation, and control of production activities, including the goods-making system, conducted by an organizational entity with defined performance objectives subject to modification according to ambient conditions.

The preparation for production consists of such activities as planning the sequence of processing, time scheduling, equipment selection, tooling, factory building construction, personnel mobilization, materials procurement, and work assignment. This preparation stage is preceded by product planning and design, which in turn derives from product research and development.

Research and development programmes are based on market surveys, pollution control studies, and forecasts of future technologies. This means that today's production management encompasses not only the management of plant level manufacturing activities but also all other preceding activities such as preparation, product planning and design, and research and development, while at the same time taking into consideration socio-economic changes.

Production management, in this sense, is not limited to the optimum management of each step, such as production or preparation for production, but calls for integrated action covering the whole spectrum of production activities which are responsive for changing circumstances and capable of increasing overall efficiency. This philosophy is synonymous with the establishment of a manufacturing system capable of quickly responding to market needs, reducing the lead time between product development and manufacturing, or the start-up period from product design to actual production. In other words, it is focused on achieving linkage between production and pre-production stages. Due to space constraints, this book deals primarily with the two phases of production and pre-production arrangements in the sequence illustrated in Figure 1-1.

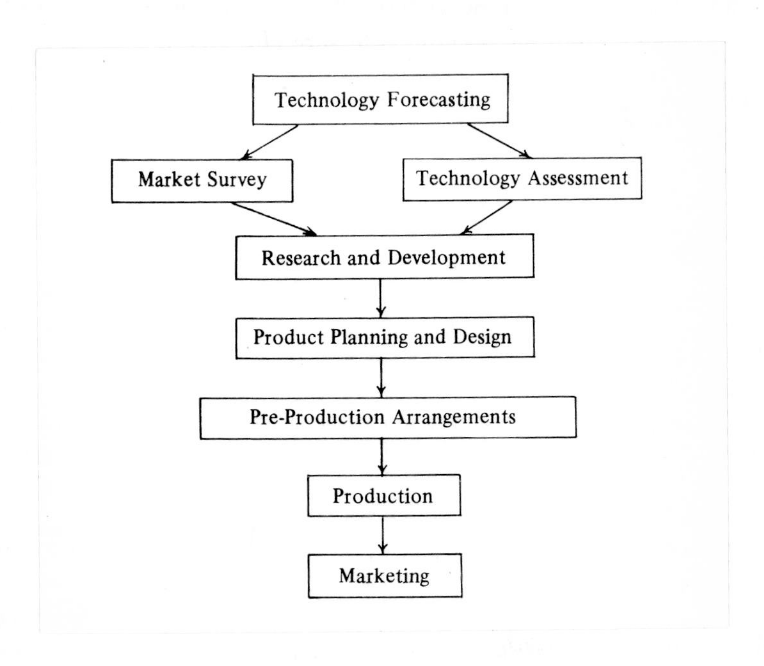

Figure 1-1 Areas of Production Management

1.2 HISTORY OF PRODUCTION MANAGEMENT

The definition of production management in the previous section is summarized by the following two points:

1) The word "production" should be interpreted to include not only the manufacturing stage but also all other stages which precede it.
2) "Management" does not merely mean control and adjustment under a prescribed set of conditions, but also implies creation of a new management system responsive to changing circumstances and selection of controls suitable in achieving corporate objectives.

There is a long history behind the establishment of such a definition.

1.2.1 Before World War II

Production management began with quality control. The basic prerequisite for modern production is the assurance of a standard of tolerance (in points) that enables interchangeability between parts and components. For instance, the cap of ball point pen A fits ball point pen B of the same brand because of the standard tolerance of points. This was made possible through mass production which began in the United States in the beginning of the 19th century. Initially, parts tolerance was controlled by means of product inspection, and this provided the basis for the sophisticated quality control techniques of today.

From the end of the 19th century to tbe beginning of the 20th century, F.W. Taylor and many others advocated labour management. The level of mechanization at that time was still rather low, so production efficiency was primarily determined by the speed at which workers operated the machines. They tried to determine the speed of operation scientifically and thus established a standard for the volume of daily operations to be performed by workers. (The actual measurement and scientific determination at the shop floor level was not an easy task.) Thus it was possible to plan to a certain degree of accuracy on the volume of work to be performed by a worker and to improve efficiency in management.

The determination of a standard volume of work made planning possible and created daily scheduling. It also started relating inventory control to daily scheduling, and one of the basic inventory decisions, economical lot size, was first modeled in 1914 (see Section 9.4 in Chapter 9). In the 1910s and 1920s, production control in the United States meant schedule and inventory control.

In the 1920s, Ford's competitors joined forces to form General Motors. Integrated management for a large number of plants was not possible through the use of conventional parameters of quality operations, daily scheduling, and inventory control. The introduction of the cost parameter as a management tool made it possible to control efficiently a number of different production formats in an integrated manner.

During the same decade, Japan and Europe began introducing this American method of controlling quality, operations, scheduling, inventory, and cost. However, that was of little help to the many corporations that went bankrupt during the Great Depression. Entrepreneurs thus came to realize the significance of profit being the difference between revenue and production cost. Reduction of cost through quality control, work scheduling, and inventory control is not enough to assure corporate profit. Revenue depends on sales and marketing which must also be emphasized.

1.2.2 After World War II

Profit-oriented production management prevailed for some time after World War II in Japan, Europe and the United States. In the 1960s, however, the concept of "corporate strategy" came into the limelight. Corporate strategy, stemming directly out of a corporation's management philosophy, may require a drastic change in the production system independently from revenue, cost, or any other parameters already in use. Particularly in this era of corporate mergers and tie-ups, the changes undergone by the the production systems needs to be covered by production management.

One noteworthy phenomenon related to production management during the course of Japan's post war recovery is the remarkable development and growth of smaller firms working as suppliers to larger corporations. Production management at the parent company had to be synchronized with the production management of its suppliers. The need for synchronization was particularly acute in Japan where larger corporations are expected to play the role of parents in the family, with suppliers assisting the parents as children of the family.

State-of-the art production management hierarchy is well exemplified in the space shuttle programme of the United States. The structuring of a gigantic pyramid of production control was possible through extensive utilization of computers. A scheduling control methodology called PERT (Programme Evaluation & Review Technique) is a typical computer application. (See Section 6.4 in Chapter 6.)

The 1970s was a decade of respect for man, with the focus on pollution control, welfare, and safety. It was a decade which demanded drastic changes in the production system and its management. New concepts, such as management by objectives and autonomous management were emphasized, and there was general recognition that the 1980's would see further progress in automation and in the delegation of management authority to people in the field. Fully-automated flexible manufacturing lines are already in operation. As a result, in the 1980s and 1990s, human labour will be employed in highly sophisticated and specialized work, thereby requiring another drastic change in production management methodology. (For evolution of production management see Figure 1-2).

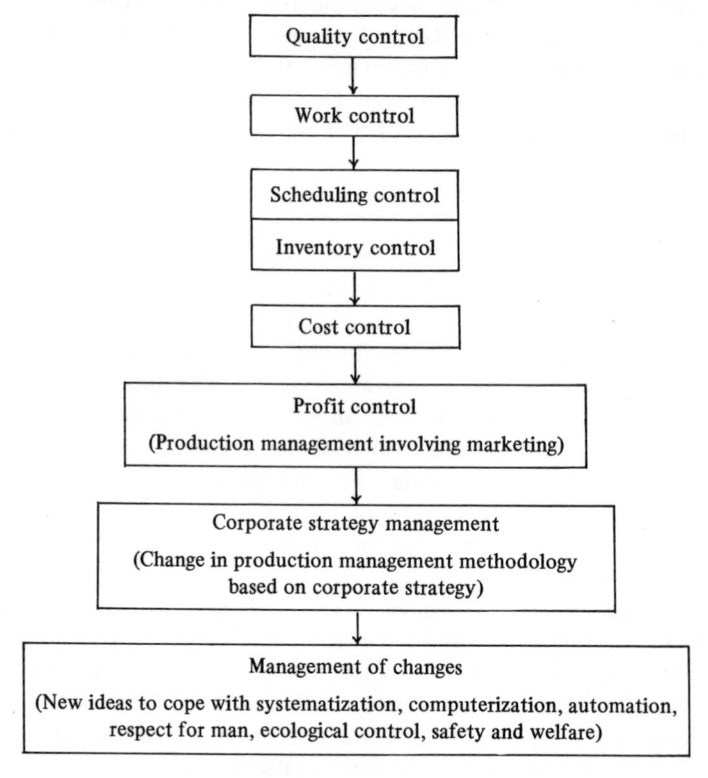

Figure 1-2 Evolution of Production Management

1.3 PRODUCTION MANAGEMENT TODAY – A SYSTEMS VIEWPOINT

Production management, which originally meant the management of production lines, has evolved into a comprehensive idea directly related to corporate strategy. The process of evolution appears to be closely related to the birth of industrial giants having complex production systems.

1.3.1 Production System Model

A production process consists of 1) objective, 2) input, 3) processing, 4) output, and 5) control and adjustment (the word "control" is used hereafter to mean both control and adjustment).

1) A clear-cut objective should first be established for any production

activity. Characteristics of the finished product should be defined together with applicable production techniques. For example, in the case of canned crab meat, the can should not be defective and should contain a specified volume/weight of crab meat, not tuna or beef. 2) "Input" refers to resources used in the production of canned crab meat, such as crab meat, wrapping paper, can, human labour, utilities, and data. 3) "Processing" means the transformation of the resources into a product which in this case is canned crab meat. Production equipment is utilized for processing. 4) "Output" is the product itself. 5) "Control" refers to the evaluation of the output with reference to the objective and to the sebsequent adjustment or modification when required.

Since the word production is defined to include production and pre-production arrangements, smooth production is not possible without proper coordination between the production and the pre-production stage. The five elements of objective, input, processing, output, and control should be deployed in a well-balanced manner not only for the production process as a whole, but also for each phase in the process such as production itself, pre-production arrangements, product planning and design, research and development, technical assessment, market survey, and technology forecasting. (See Figure 1-3). In other words, a favourable relationship should be maintained between input and output throughout the entire production process. A favourable relationship in this case is defined as a relationship which realizes the fixed objective with the use of minimum resources.

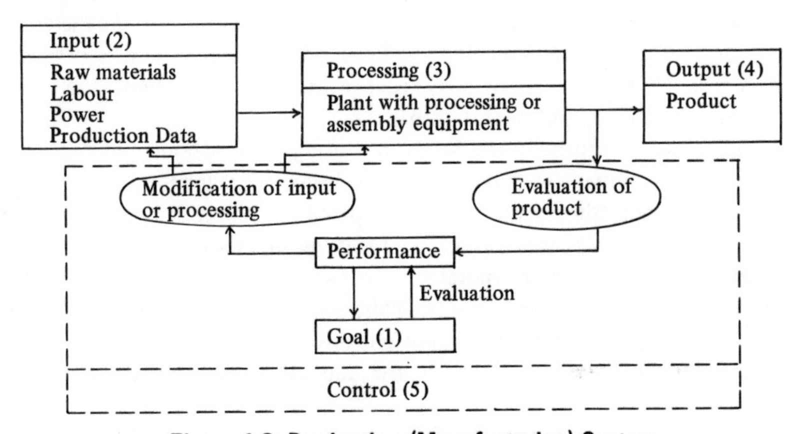

Figure 1-3 Production (Manufacturing) System

Note: This diagram is not only applicable to each phase preceding production, it is also applicable to the entire cycle beginning with technology forecasting and ending with production. The numerals in the diagram correspond to those in the text.

1.3.2 Characteristics of Production System

Let us take a look at the general characteristics of a production system consisting primarily of input and output. Here, "production system" does not have the wider connotation involving all the phases from technology forecasting to manufacturing. "Production system" is used in the narrow sense of the term, and all other phases which belong to the production system in the wider sense are considered part of the production environment. This definition process is called "system discrimination".

When discussing a production system in the narrow sense, however, one cannot ignore its relationship with other phases of the broader production system. The closed relationship that exists between production and pre-production arrangements is known as the "inter-relationship" between systems.

A production system, when identified with a manufacturing firm, consists of the headquarters, administrative department, factory, and production field, all forming the strata of corporate hierarchy. Each stratum has its specific role to play depending on the size of the firm and enjoys benefits as a result of its performance. As pointed out by Adam Smith, the integration of specialized functions brings about maximum results. This means that as the production system expands, it tends to have larger numbers of hierarchial strata performing specialized functions.

A production system is characterized by discrimination, interrelationship, stratum formation, and specialization, which is the basis for today's corporate organization. There are two more general characteristics inherent in a production system: (1) the system needs to have a constant input flow of new energy in order to keep on functioning and (2) ways and means of reaching goals may change from time to time, thereby affecting the input-output relationship.

If a manufacturing firm stops recruiting high school and college graduates, its human resources tend to become stagnant for obvious reasons. The same theory applies to equipment. Without the replacement of old machines with new ones, the firm's production facility becomes obsolete and inefficient. Corporate organization also needs rejuvenation. Otherwise its function deteriorates. This deterioration process has been called the increase of entropy, where entropy is a measure of the degradation of the matter and energy in the universe to an ultimate state of inert uniformity.

There are a number of different mechanisms applicable to the input-output relationship in a production system. Let us take the auto industry as an example. Toyota makes use of a large number of suppliers as an *infrastructure* to its production system. General Motors emphasizes in-house parts supply so that its purchases from outside are basically on an ad hoc contractural basis with independent suppliers. Although these two corporations have an identical objective of efficient car production, Toyota takes a route that is different from General Motors' due to the peculiar economic environment in Japan. This process of reaching the same goal by different routes is called "iso-finality."

Among the characteristics discussed, the obsolescence of equipment and organization needs particular attention. As time goes by, entropy increases within the corporate structure, thereby deteriorating its function. In this era of profound changes and dramatic technological innovations, the need for rejuvenation cannot be over-emphasized. If production management is to be called on to cope dynamically with this situation, it should be prepared to rejuvenate itself.

1.4 PRODUCTION MANAGEMENT TODAY – TWO TYPES OF CONTROL

The input-processing-output relation should be controlled regardless of the size of the production system. Systematic control should also be applied to the production system in its broader sense from technology forecasting to production. In all cases, control is the basis for production management.

There are two types of production system control, feedback and feedforward. (Figure 1-4 is referred.)

The feedback type corresponds to the control phase at the bottom of Figure 1-3. Output is obtained as a result of input and processing, and is measured using a measuring instrument. In the example of canned crab meat, the product is weighed. If the weight of the product is in agreement with the goal or specification, the production line continues to operate without modification.

On the other hand, if the weight of the product is substantially different from the goal, adjustment is made in processing and/or input. The necessity for such adjustment is determined with reference to the control chart based on the theory of statistical quality control (see Section 6-5 in Chapter 6). The result of the measurement is seldom in complete agreement with the goal. Therefore, specifications normally have tolerances, such as ±5/1000 milimeters. Line adjustment is initiated when a statistically meaningful number of products fall outside the tolerance range. This is called the principle of exception, a popular expression in business management.

In the case of the feedforward type control, input is checked against a prescribed formula prior to the 'processing' and 'output' phases. Unlike feedback type control, poor output is subject to modification prior to the check on final products.

At Toyota, every work station is equipped with a "Bakayoke" which detects and physically removes defects in an automated fashion. The next work station downstream can rest assured that all the materials it receives satisfied specifications. Preventive maintenance is a kind of feedforward control. The life of each critical machine component is determined, and those components are replaced before their life runs out. Proper training of recruits on preventive maintenace is also an effective way of assuring feedforward control.

Figure 1-4 shows a typical feedforward control diagram. In order to assure smooth operation of such a control, a tailor-made control system should be established with a clear-cut definition of control parameters and specifications. The control system automatically collects measurement data, compares them against the specification and initiates modification on input when the need arises. In a production system, both feedback and feedforward controls may be used simultaneously for attaining economic efficiency.

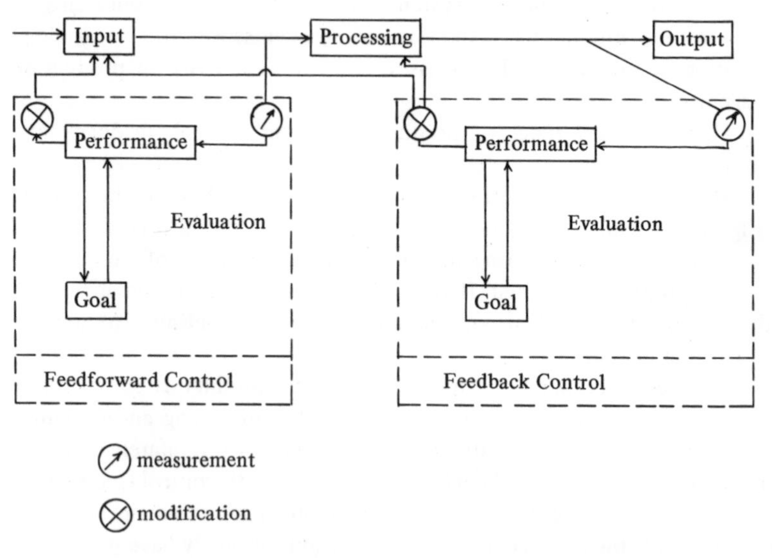

Figure 1-4 Two Types of Control in a Production System

1.5 PRODUCTION MANAGEMENT TODAY – PRODUCTIVITY IMPROVEMENT

Production management sees that products fall within a certain tolerance range with reference to the specification. Specifications tend to change and become tighter so the product may remain competitive in the face of accelerating technological advancements. Corporations must change their production systems in order to survive. The Japanese manufacturing industry gained its international competitiveness as a result of drastic changes in the production field.

Those who last visited a manufacturing plant before 1975, should go back to the same plant and see what has happened since then. The work space is well-lit, clean, and quiet with very few people present. And yet, productivity has improved many fold through extensive use of computers and sophisticated machines. Manpower-oriented manufacturing belongs to the past.

This evolution was necessary due to severe competition in the market. Production management has responded to the inexhaustible demand for higher productivity on the part of the production system. What is productivity, then? Productivity is a function of the relationship between production input and output. Productivity improves when a given output is achieved with less input or a given input results in a larger output.

Both input and output can be expressed in terms of energy units. There is material energy which represents raw materials and equipment and mental energy representing brainwork. Productivity improves when waste is either decreased or eliminated, materially or mentally so that a larger percentage of energy input is obtained as output.

Figure 1-4 shows the role of production management is twofold. One is to make certain performance satisfies the production goal, and the other is to modify the production goal to suit the change in technology and demand in the market. The Japanese manufacturing industry acquired its competitiveness through simultaneous application of these two types of production management. In the Japanese manufacturing plant, upgrading of the production goal is initiated by field workers who then make a concerted effort to realize such a goal. In other words, production management is field worker oriented or autonomous.

The idea of productivity improvement through production management is also applicable to other industries such as wholesaling, retailing and service. Taxpayers are pleased when government offices, schools and hospitals improve their service through production management. The concept of production management was born and nurtured within the framework of the manufacturing industry. The function of production management, defined as the fulfillment and refinement of performance goals, is geared towards universal applications in industries other than manufacturing. That is why the expression "operations management" is often used instead of production management. Recently, researchers are rigorously studying its applications to achieve productivity improvement in the service industry.

This is a logical evolution because it is possible to systematically control operations in the service industry in terms of the input-processing-output sequence. Today's production management technology is rapidly expanding its applications in industries other than manufacturing. Input-output relations exist in any project. If one attempts to minimize input and maximize output, it becomes necessary to place the whole sequence of input-processing-production under control. The Japanese manufacturing industry did exactly that. The result was effective utilization of human and natural resources. The author thinks Japan is on the right track.

Chapter 2
PRODUCTION FORMAT AND MANAGEMENT

No matter how advanced production technologies may be, production format is solely governed by the production of output, measured in products or services. It is not necessary to set up a large scale flow production line to manufacture just one unit of a product. In this chapter four different production formats will be defined according to production lot size.

2.1 CLASSIFICATION OF PRODUCTION FORMATS

2.1.1 Four Representative Formats

There are five typical methods of categorization. The simplest way to classify production formats is by lot size, namely, single-unit production, small lot production, medium lot production, large lot production, and continuous production. This is an effective means of classification as it clarifies the difference in the status of production. But it also has some demerits. It is difficult to establish a clear-cut distinction among small, medium, and large lot sizes in on-going operations. Furthermore, lot size is also a function of product size, weight, and the type of processing applied.

The second method of classification is to determine whether the production process is continuous or intermittent. This is apparently a simpler method compared with the first one, but completely ignores lot size or the scope of production. Therefore, this is not a suitable method for analytical purposes.

The third classification method is related to the number of product types and production lot sizes. This classification comprises three categories, namely, small-scale production of a large variety of products, medium-scale production of a limited range of products, and large-scale production of a small variety of products. This method takes market conditions into consideration and is an effective means of analyzing modern production management. Then, how is this method different from the first one?

Technological conditions being equal, a larger production lot results in a lower production cost per unit. However, demand in the market does not always warrant large lot production. The recent trend is for small-scale production of a large variety of products, or *flexible manufacturing.* Manufacturers try to cope with diversification in market demand through standardization of production lines, thereby maximizing the sizes of the production lot per type.

In the case of car production, a standard engine may be mounted on various vehicles with different body shapes and functions. A communal stamping design is created for similar applications in the vehicle. In this way, the production lot size for that particular stamping can be expanded although production lots per vehicle type may be smaller. This methodology is called *standardization of component* or *group technology.*

The fourth classification is related to order booking. This method comprises job order production and production to stock. The first category applies generally to small lot production while the latter to large lot or continuous production. A typical example of production to stock is ski equipment which enjoys demand only during the winter season, although its production may go on throughout the year. Discrepancies between demand estimation and actual orders received for the season are adjusted in terms of increase or decrease in product inventory. In the case of job order production, however, fluctuation in order bookings directly affects production layout in terms of work force and equipment utilization, resulting in relocations and lay-offs in extreme cases. In actual operation, both types of production are used interchangeably depending on the trend in the market. The comparison among the four classifications is in Figure 2-1.

2.1.2 Other Classifications

A production format may be classified in terms of the size of the production system expressed through the number of employees or the amount of fixed assets involved. In terms of the number of employees, 20 or less means a small production unit, 21 to 300 is medium-small, 301 to 1,000 means medium and 1,001 or more may be called a large production unit. A production unit employing more than 10,000 people may be called a giant corporation.

How does the size of a production system affect the production format? In the case of small-scale production, the format is normally single-unit or small lot production in one location without a sales organization. Small and medium sized firms are compatible with medium lot and large lot production. Medium and large sized corporations normally employ large lot continuous production formats. In some exceptional cases, such as manufacturers of heavy power generators, the assembly work is intermittent and in single-unit small lot production even at medium and large sized corporations. A giant corporation normally has a number of production units, occasionally including those in foreign countries, and their production formats may be different from factory to factory.

In recent years, demand in the market has become increasingly diversified and small in quantity, forcing giant corporations to modify their production formats. As a result, continuous production is no longer the predominant format employed by giant corporations and is being replaced by small and medium lot production. The general trend is for small-scale production of a large variety of products.

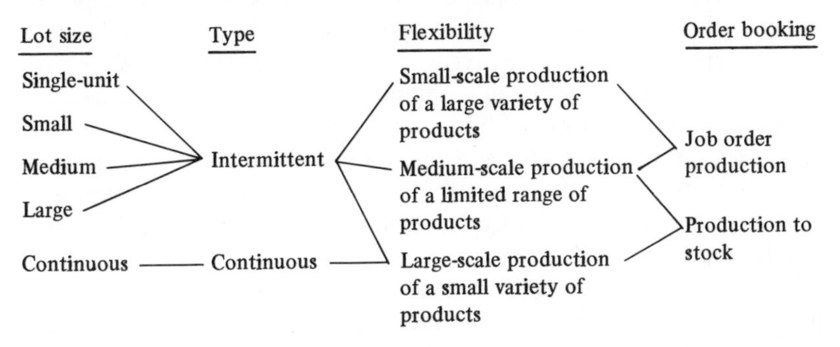

Figure 2-1 Classification of Production Formats

In large corporations with several production units, there are well-developed organization for pre-production arrangements such as preparation for production, product planning and design, and research and development. These arrangements are project-oriented and compatible with single-unit, small lot production. Smaller corporations that specialize in manufacturing are often dependent on outside help such as their parent companies, machine manufacturers, suppliers of raw materials, customers, and consultants for such pre-production arrangements.

Another production format requiring particular attention in Japan is subcontracting. Subcontractors, or parts suppliers, are not merely outside vendors but constitute an integral part of the overall production format. Optimum production is not possible without a well-balanced supplier control.

A classification is also possible between stable and non-stable production. The non-stable production requires frequent line changes reflecting changing needs in the market whereas stable production seldom calls for line changes.

There are other special formats applicable to prototype production, pilot run, field maintenance, spare parts production, and the production of jigs, fixtures and samples. A comprehensive production format analysis should include such special cases in addition to normal factory production. Basic production formats apply also to pre-production arrangements for which single-unit, small lot production formats are often utilized.

2.2 CHARACTERISTICS OF PRODUCTION FORMATS

2.2.1 Single-Unit and Small Lot Production

Workers with multi-faceted ability are required in a single-unit, small lot production format, as they have to tackle various kinds of work, one after another. Although a long training period is required, the worker is motivated because the acquired knowledge or skills can be employed instantly. Production and transport equipment should be compatible with various types of work and be ready for flexible applications. Work flow is basically irregular with let-ups, collisions, and reverse flows. Therefore, particular attention is required for inventory control.

This format is not used exclusively by small production units. Large manufacturing corporations use it for their pre-production arrangements such as preparation for production, product planning, design, and research and development.

Small manufacturing firms use this format all the way from pre-production arrangements to final production. Since innovative products are a key to success in the world of business, single-unit, small lot production formats for all pre-production arrangements need particular attention, regardless of the size of the production system.

2.2.2 Continuous Production

Continuous production in process type work is different from that in an assembly industry. In the assembly type, continuous production without automation means mass utilization of human labour for simple repetitive work, bringing about a de-humanization of workers. In the process type, workers are physically away from the equipment except for maintenance. They simply monitor instruments and make proper adjustments when necessary.

Instruments for process type work are highly sophisticated and operate as a system rather than piece by piece. Such systems have been subject to computer control for many years. On the other hand, automation and the introduction of robotics in the assembly line are relatively recent phenomena implemented for limited applications. Assembly work is still heavily dependent on manual labour, leaving much room for improvement.

Each assembly line is dedicated to certain types of products and is therefore conveyor-compatible. Work flow should be kept smooth and inventory between work stations subject to rigid control. Synchronization is attained among work stations by means of work balancing or the equalization of work time per station or per worker.

Strictly speaking, however, continuous production is subject to certain interruptions because each product has a finite life. At the present rate of technological change, product life is becoming shorter every year, making product-dedicated equipment vulnerable to rapid obsolescence. That is why high-priced durable equipment should be so designed as to accommodate minor modifications. This phenomenon may be called the *generalization* of product-dedicated equipment. The same consideration is applicable to the entire production line. For instance, one engine assembly line can be designed to handle several different engines from time to time without changing its basic layout.

2.2.3 Medium and Large Lot Production

Medium and large lot production falls between small lot production and continuous production. Here, the worker's job is neither simple and repetitive nor extremely multi-faceted. Machine utilization is half specialized and half generalized. Work flow is not so smooth as in continuous production but more continuous than in the case of small lot production. The lot size requires organized production.

Automation is being vigorously introduced in this production format for material handling, processing and inspection. Automation is a proven means of cost reduction for certain processes. As a result, this production format is gaining dominance over continuous production. This is a logical choice for smaller manufacturing firms whose products have enjoyed a sudden boost in sales.

On the other hand, efforts are being made to convert single-unit small lot production to medium or large lot production through standardization and sharing of parts and equipment. Technological conditions being equal, a larger production lot means a lower production cost per unit, realized through the saving in set-up time and the accumulation of expertise on the part of workers. However, in some cases, the production lot is scaled down in size or broken up to reduce inventory or to shorten the delivery period.

2.3 PRODUCTION FORMAT AND ITS MANAGEMENT

Production management is executed differently depending on the production format. In single-unit production, time scheduling requires rigid control in order to realize smooth work flow, as found in aircraft production, space satellite assembly, and large building construction. A scheduling control technology called PERT is often used for such large projects. (See Section 6-4 in Chapter 6.)

The most important control parameter for medium and large lot production is inventory. Lot-by-lot line inventory should be maintained at low levels. In large lot production, an inventory of half-finished products between work stations should be rigorously controlled. In some cases, it may be advisable to split a large production lot into several medium lots to avoid excessive inventory accumulation, remembering the importance of line allocation for different lot sizes.

What about continuous production? In the case of process type production, particularly when based on chemical reaction, it is virtually impossible to change the speed of production. Production, therefore, should be controlled and managed in terms of equipment utilization and the number of working hours per day or week. In the case of assembly type production, production speed can be controlled to a certain extent. In both cases, production should be managed to satisfy the changing demand in the market.

The following different formats are applicable to different types of production:

1) Special project control, 2) order control, 3) load control, 4) block control, and 5) flow control, all of which are implemented inhouse, and 6) supplier control which goes beyond the boundaries of one parent corporation. Special project control is for complex single-unit production. Order control is normally suited for single unit, small lot production. Likewise, load control, block control and flow control are applied to medium, large and continuous production formats, respectively. Supplier control is exercised with consideration of the supplier's production format.

In special project control, time, labour, cost, and technology are used as control parameters. This control technique is suitable primarily for 1) fabrication and assembly of large-sized products of complex design, 2) major modification of production systems, and 3) large-scale pre-production arrangements.

Order control is applicable to small lot, single unit production by order which is non-repetitive. Delicate non-repetitive type pre-production arrangement may also be suited to this type of management.

Load control is directed towards production bottlenecks. As mentioned before, inventory control is of vital importance for medium and large lot production. Therefore, bottleneckes are identified and assessed in terms of semi-finished product inventories between work stations. Load control aims at optimizing the work load so inventories between work stations will be reduced or eliminated.

Block control breaks a large production lot into blocks which are identified by number. It is a pseudo flow control applied only to large production lots.

Flow control is related to flow planning and execution as the name implies. The management technique is meaningful only in the case of demand-pull type production.

Supplier control needs to be implemented in conjunction with the aforementioned five management techniques. Optimal integration of inhouse production management and supplier control is indispensable for survival in this era of severe competition.

A large and complex production system tends to require a large and complex management system. As discussed in Chapter 1, production management constantly demands improvement in quality, work, time, quantity, and cost. It also calls for co-ordination between marketing and production, coupled with the improvement of production management techniques in compliance with changes in business strategy and environment. As the production system grows in scale and complexity, so does production management.

Improvement in pre-production arrangements further complicates production systems. Pre-production arrangements are also subject to production management. Production management should cover a large number of elements throughout the long production sequence yet should remain simple in order to avoid redundancy and an excessive financial burden. (See Figure 2-2.)

2.4 PRODUCTION FORMATS FOR SMALL AND MEDIUM-SIZED FIRMS

Production formats such as single-unit, small lot production, intermittent production, small scale production of a large variety of products, and job order production are considered to be compatible with small and medium-sized firms (See Figure 2-1). In the production management format, order control and load control are used in most cases. Since the majority of small and medium-sized firms serve as suppliers to larger corporations, they are subject to supplier control by larger corporations or parent companies. (See Figure 2-2.)

Parameters used for production management by smaller firms include quality, work, time, quantity, cost, profit, new product strategy, and environment. Production management should be simple and effective. As for product quality, the satisfaction of the customers' purchasing specifications should be the objective. Production management determines the optimal yield and the technologies required to fulfil that objective. Statistical quality control techniques may be used for this purpose. (See

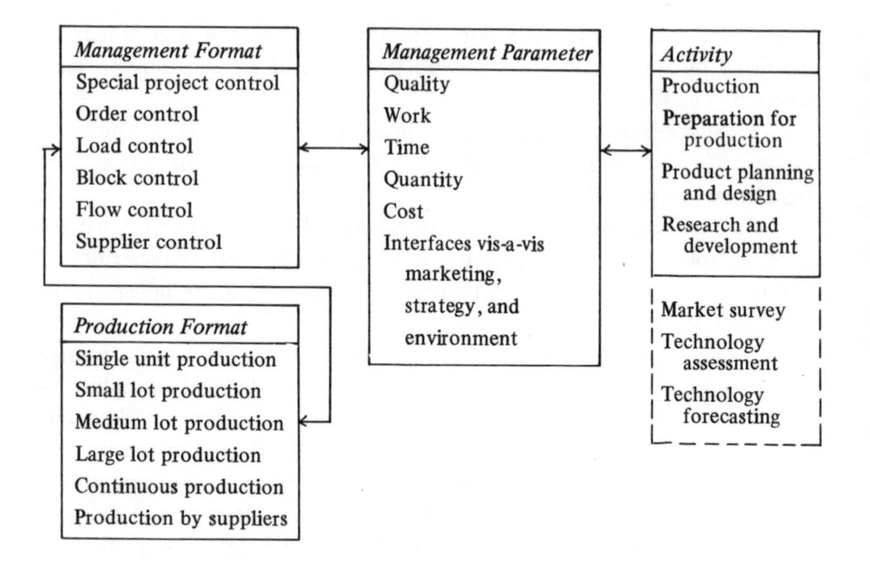

Figure 2-2 Production Management Formats

Activities in the dotted frame are theoretically categorized as a part of production but not subject to production management.

All production formats are related to inhouse production with the exception of production by suppliers, which is external.

Section 6.5 of Chapter 6.)

Human labour comes first in the work parameter, although automation through introduction of the so-called *mechatronics* equipment, including computers, has wrought dramatic changes in production control, primarily in terms of work standardization. Still the training of human labour, in the broad sense of the word, is the linchpin even for automation (See Chapters 3 and 4).

The control is a matter of life and death to small and medium-sized firms. Their customers constantly ask for improvement in the delivery period and in service for their products. Those who fail to comply with such requests may drop out of business. Small and medium-sized firms need to have simple and effective time management in order to survive. (See Chapters 6 and 9.)

Quantity control means inventory control. Since smaller production units are normally engaged in small-scale production of a large variety of products, special care must be taken in the reduction of inventory of partially finished products. Smooth production with minimal inventory is synonymous with drastic cost reduction. Smaller manufacturing firms should pay due attention to quantity control in order to improve their competitiveness. (See Chapters 6, 9, and 10.)

In terms of production cost control, what is basically needed for smaller firms is an all-out effort at cost reduction rather than the implementation of cost control systems. This book focuses on the relationship between production management and sales as a means of revenue generation, particularly the application of production management pertaining to quality, work, time, quantity, and cost. Section 6-2 in Chapter 6 primarily deals with this problem.

Production management that responds to changes in corporate strategy and the business environment is important for smaller firms as well as larger corporations. This subject will be further discussed in Chapter 5. Changes in corporate strategy and business environment force changes in production management. Production management should be flexible enough to accommodate such changes.

Finally, systematization is important. As pointed out elsewhere in this book, there is a growing need for production management of pre-production arrangements including preparation for production, product planning and design, irrespective of the size of the corporation. In the case of smaller firms, proper coordination with their parent companies, customers, and vendors is necessary. Flexible implementation of appropriate production management methodology is required on an ad-hoc basis.

Chapter 3
PRODUCTION MANAGEMENT, AUTOMATION AND COMPUTERIZATION

Automation and computerization are in the limelight. This Chapter describes the significance of automation and computers in the production field and their impact on production management. It also deals with automation and computerization from the standpoint of economic efficiency.

3.1 FROM MANUAL TO MACHINE PROCESSING

Automation and computerization are likely to bring about drastic changes in the "work" element of production management. In the beginning of the 20th Century, production management essentially meant the scientific management of human "work." Presently, however, the work element has a different connotation. Automation through aggressive utilization of machinery and computers has appreciably pervaded virtually all industries including the service industry.

Let us assume a completely automated production line. The material is fed automatically to the line and correctly positioned for processing. After processing, the material is automatically removed and inspected for delivery to the next production line.

Such a production line or machine is no longer a rare phenomenon even in smaller manufacturing plants, let alone large corporations engaged in large lot production. Here, work control means control of machines and control of the equipment utilization rate, rather than control of conventional workers' operations.

The equipment utilization rate is defined as the percentage ratio between the full processing capacity of the equipment and the processing capacity in use. If a machine which is capable of processing at 1,000 r.p.m. is used at 750 r.p.m., its utilization rate is 75%. Due to technological innovations and severe competition, production machines are expected to be used to their full production capacity. A machine which is designed for processing at 2,000 r.p.m. should always be operating at 2,000 r.p.m. Equipment utilization rate in this case is 100%.

In the real world, however, the machine stops from time to time due to set-up, break down of the machine in operation, and temporary absence of work pieces. Smaller production lots require frequent line changes, thereby reducing operation time of the machine. A broken bit, loose placement of the work piece, foreign objects, or a defective work piece are among the causes for machine shut down, which diminishes the equipment utilization rate. A poor interface with work stations upstream is also a cause for shut down since the machine would temporarily have no work piece. The following equation mathematically defines the equipment utilization rate:

$$\text{Equipment utilization rate (\%)} = \frac{\text{Machine's net operational period of time}}{\text{Operational period of time}}$$

$$= \frac{\text{Operational period of time} - \text{Set-up time} - \text{Shut down time due to breakdown} - \text{Queue time due to poor interface}}{\text{Operational period of time}} \times 100$$

The manager of machine operations formulates a production plan based on the equipment utilization rate and calculated on the actual performance of the machine. Afterwards, he endeavours to improve the utilization rate primarily through shorter set-up times which allow high utilization rates, even for small production lots resulting from the present trend towards multiple variety, small lot production.

Second, the operations manager endeavours to reduce down-time through the employment of industrial engineering techniques. The amount of energy dedicated to this end is far beyond laymen's imagination. Production fields themselves are now storehouses of know-how on machine operation.

Third, the manager endeavours to maintain a smooth work flow so materials are always available where they are needed, when they are needed, and in the right quantities. Optimal work flow is obtained through proper time and quantity control. Quality control is also required because the elimination of defective parts in the production line drastically reduces down-time.

To summarize, efficient machine operation is possible through 1) shorter set-up time, 2) machine down-time reduction, and 3) smooth material supply. Improvement in equipment utilization rates can be attained in a variety of ways, each requiring a great deal of effort. Due to automation, today's production management is machine-oriented rather than worker-oriented. Production machines are dealt with as integrated systems rather than groups of individual machines. A machine which incorporates different functions such as automatic feeding, processing, removal, and inspection may be considered a production system in itself.

3.2 AUTOMATION AND PRODUCTION MANAGEMENT

3.2.1 Progress in Automation

Automation began in Cleveland, Ohio in 1946, when Ford's Cleveland plant introduced transfer machines. In order to reduce set-up time in continuous processing, Ford automated a complete process line for certain components by introducing machines capable of doing material handling, aligning, and processing without human intervention. It was not long before automation began to infiltrate into small scale production of a large variety of products. Numerically-controlled machine tools appeared in the U.S.A. in 1952. The first numerically-controlled (N/C) machine tool produced in Japan made its debut six years later in 1958. The machining centre, a complex processing structure consisting of more than one N/C machine tool, was introduced in the U.S.A. in 1958 and in Japan in 1960.

Complete factory automation (FA) was possible through the aggressive use of N/C machines and machining centres. Robotics also played a vital role in automation. Robotics were reportedly used in the manufacturing industry of the United States in 1958. Japan began to manufacture robots domestically in 1968. Unlike N/C machines and machining centres, robots are capable of doing flexible three-dimensional movement. The current trend in automation is to establish an integrated operational system comprising N/C machine tools, machining centres, and robots through computerization. Such a production system is called a flexible manufacturing system (FMS). Automation also took place in product designing. The combination of computer aided designing and manufacturing systems, called CAD/CAM, is expected to be used extensively in the 1980s.

3.2.2 Impact on Production Management

The most conspicuous impact presents itself in machine control. As discussed in the previous chapter, independent control devices can be incorporated into small machines. With the inspection function, for instance, the machine could automatically compare every processed work piece with the standard piece to see if work specifications are satisfied. If not, the machine stops by itself and sets off an alarm at the control centre for human intervention. In this case, the routine part of machine control is all done by the machine itself. Human intervention is necessary only for correction purposes.

How does FMS affect production management? In FMS, most time control is done by computer, but the physical loading of work pieces on pallets is done by people. After pallet loading, the load information is conveyed from the terminal at the loading station to the Central Processing Unit (CPU). The CPU in turn computes the load, evaluates the load against the work in progress for each machine in operation, and makes assignments (work pieces loaded on a pallet). An automatic transport picks up the pallet, carries it to the machine, unloads the parts, and carries the pallet back to the pallet yard. Everything is done by computer and machine, except preparation for processing, machine maintenance, and emergency actions. The basic programme and modifications of FMS are, of course, done manually, which adds sophistication to human labour.

Quantity control, particularly line inventory control, in FMS can be conducted semi-automatically by restricting the area space for set-up and limiting the number of stock pools beside the production line. Further inventory reduction is attainable through an increase in processing speed and shortening of set-up time. Proper attention should be paid to reduce shut-down time of the machine during operation.

Cost control should be based on the viability assessment at the time of FMS installation. Once FMS is installed, optimal operation should be maintained to realize low production cost. The profitability of FMS is greatly affected by market demand and should be considered prior to its introduction.

3.3 COMPUTERIZATION AND PRODUCTION MANAGEMENT

Time and quantity controls belong to the computer domain, particularly in the case where complex processing is required on a variety of work pieces grouped together in small lots.

Figure 3-1 illustrates the sequence of computer control. Planning and control related to scheduling and inventory are performed using computers. Accurate information should be gathered and updated from time to time to reflect technological innovation. A communal data base should be set up and shared by all mini and micro-computers within the corporate structure. Coordination is important to safeguard against redundancy and inefficient organization.

Material requirements planning (MRP) in Figure 3-1 calls item-by-item computation of the quantities of raw materials required for the production of a desired quantity of the product specified in the "rough production schedule." This computation uses material analysis data on one or a small number of the products as co-efficients. Needless to say, stock on hand should be deducted from demand to arrive at the required production quantity. Then, the existing production facility is checked against the required production quantity. If they are not in agreement, the rough production schedule should be corrected. If they do agree, the detailed production plan is formed and implemented, and performance is controlled against the plan.

In the implementation and control phases in Figure 3-1, corporations belonging to the Toyota group apply the so-called "Kan-ban" system. In this system, a computer prints out daily material requirements to control the flow of materials for the coming month. Field supervisors issue X number of Kan-ban (which literally means sign) based on the print-out data. Workers themselves control the flow of materials and products from the receiving point to delivery according to the instructions on Kan-ban. The "Kan-ban" system is a type of production management that emphasizes motivated participation by field workers. Human control, not computer, is the key to encouraging suggestions for the improvement of productivity. A computer simply processes input data; it cannot be creative. (The "Kan-ban" system is discussed in Section 10-2 of Chapter 10 and in the appendix at the end of the book.)

The weakness of computer control lies in the lack of methodological improvement at the work site which can only be initiated and implemented by the workers themselves. This is where training of the workers to inspire their participation becomes necessary.

In addition to time and quantity control, computers wield power in QC systems design, data collection, data processing, computation, and communication. Work control uses computers for job standardization and for the generation of work orders based on daily production schedules.

Computers play an important role in cost and profit control. In the case of large corporations, efficient data collection, processing, computation, and communication are possible only through the use of computers.

Production management finds computers can be utilized in starting-up new products. Computer can plan and execute product design, model making, testing, time control, initial equipment investment, parts procurement, line layout, and job description. Computers establish coordination between all these phases of product development and thereby eliminate idle time, shorten lead time, and reduce the number of work steps.

Here again, the gathering of information is of vital importance in obtaining consensus and coordination among all parties related to product development. Computerization of production management should be implemented at the proper time, place, and occasion. Despite its limitations, the computer will grow into an indispensable tool for production management. Corporations, therefore, should take an aggressive stance towards computerization for their own sake and to serve the community at large.

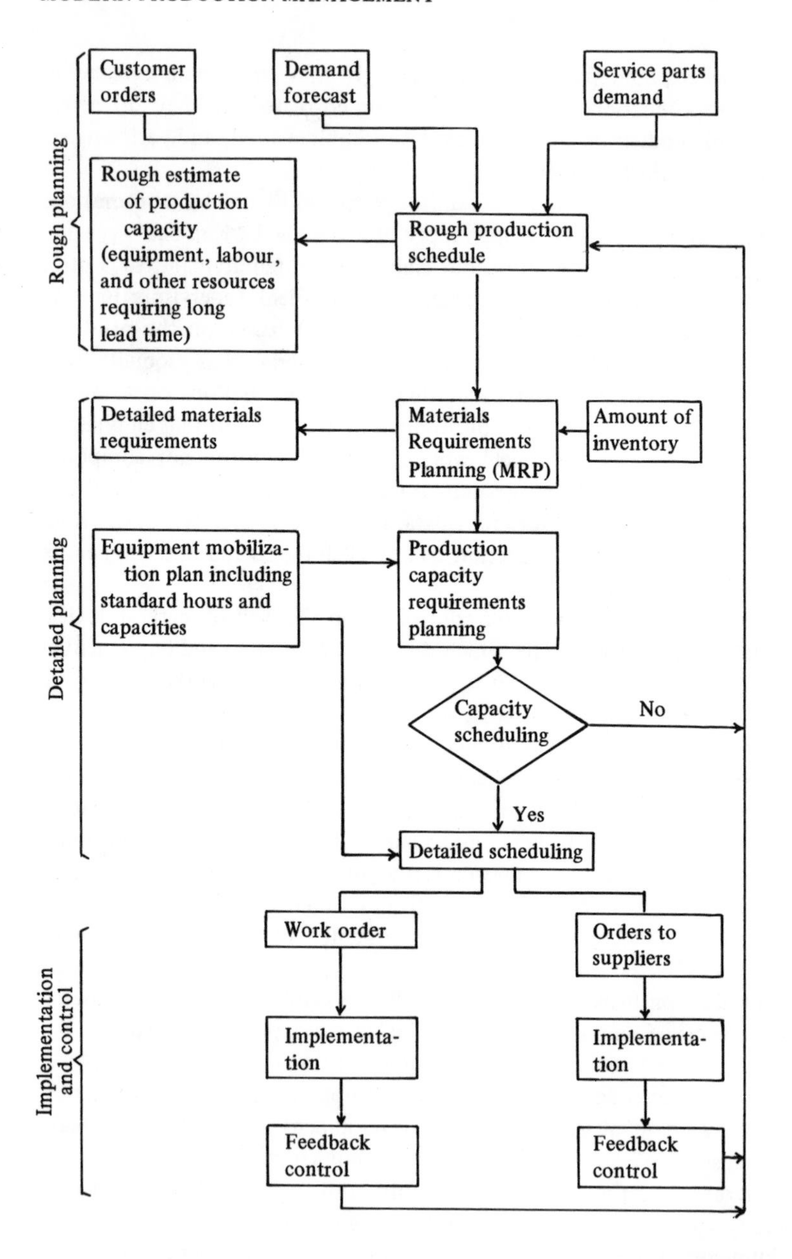

Figure 3-1 Feed-Back Type Scheduling and Inventory Control

Source: Franklin G. Moore and Thomas E. Hendrick; *Production Operations Management,* 8th Edition, Irwin, 1980, p. 332

3.4 ECONOMIC EFFICIENCY OF AUTOMATION AND COMPUTERIZATION

3.4.1 Four Basic Factors

The first factor to be considered, the necessity of acquiring new techniques, is becoming increasingly important with recent technological innovations. Elementary school children and junior high school students learn quickly how to use personal computers, whereas people in their fifties find them difficult to master. As one gets older, it becomes increasingly difficult to learn something new.

Many new techniques have to be mastered in order to operate machining centres and robots. These new production devices are technically more sophisticated than computers, and a large amount of software knowledge is required to operate such complex machines and systems. Time and money required to acquire this knowledge many be categorized as a type of equipment investment. If the inhouse creation of software proves to be too costly, management may decide to buy it elsewhere. The purchasing cost in this case can also be categorized as equipment investment.

The second factor to be considered is obsolescence of equipment. The faster the technological advancement, the greater the danger of obsolescence. The utilization of leasing systems is a convenient way of minimizing such a danger. Computerization and automation make it possible to operate machines twenty four hours a day, thereby accelerating amortization and shortening the life of equipment (independently from the statutory depreciation).

The third factor is the relationship between cost saving and profit. Sales price can be reduced to the extent of cost reduction to meet competition. Therefore, automation does not boost profit in the long run. A manufacturer accomplishing automation ahead of competitors can enjoy profit only until the competitors automate their own production. These three factors significantly affect the economic merits of automation and computerization.

The last factor is maintenance. The more sophisticated automation is, the more complex maintenance becomes. A decision must be made as to whether the maintenance is to be made inhouse or by outside parties. In both cases, preventive maintenance is important. Spare parts should be readily available for emergencies in order to minimize idle time of th machine. Maintenance and its management are becoming increasingly important.

3.4.2 Computation of Economic Efficiency

There are three equations used to quantify the merits of automation and computerization. However, decision making on automation-related investment in real life is not that easy.

Return on investment is the key parameter for any investment. The amount of procurable investment funds may be limited or unlimited. When unlimited funding is available, investment is viable for net present values (NPV) greater than zero. The larger NPV is the preferred investment.

$$NPV = \sum_{t=1}^{n} \frac{Rt}{(1+K)^t} - C_o$$

where, R_t is the total profit generated during period t
n is the life of equipment
C_o is the amount of initial investment
K is the return on alternative investment (market rate of interest is often used instead to simplify the calculation).

Positive NPV means that the investment under evaluation is more profitable than the alternative, which is profitable at the rate of K.

For a known amount of investment, priority is determined by return on investment (ROI).

$$ROI = \sum_{t=1}^{n} \frac{R_t}{(1+K)^t} / C_o$$

The notation is the same as given previously.

The above two equations are based on the assumption that profit is measurable. In actual practice, however, it is extremely difficult to estimate the profit generated by automation. In the face of rapid technological advances, entrepreneurs often use the recovery period method instead for estimation purposes. The recovery period means the number of months or years required to recover investment using the profit for redemption. The calculation is very simple, if one ignores interest. If a robot costing ten million yen replaces a worker earning five million yen a year, the recovery period is two years. In the case of present value being taken into consideration, the solution of the following equation for "x" is the recovery period.

$$\sum_{t=1}^{x} \frac{R_t}{(1+K)^t} = C_o$$

This methodology gives a realistic solution to the problem of evaluating short-term risky investments.

3.5 AUTOMATION AND COMPUTERIZATION BY SMALL AND MEDIUM-SIZED FIRMS

Generally speaking, small and medium-sized firms do not have much technological expertise. That does not mean they can avoid automation, only that they should seek economical automation and computerization. Low-cost automation may be within their reach as it requires moderate investment but does not require drastic changes in production technologies. After implementing this low-cost automation, they can then look for more sophisticated production technology. Low-cost automation is not for re-structuring the entire production system, only that portion affected.

Automation and computerization bring about drastic changes in corporate management. More than ever, small and medium-sized firms are in need of production management for pre-production arrangements. Automation and computerization demand intensive employee training or technology transfer for the operation of sophisticated machinery. Technology transfer is not possible without capable management.

Technology is transferred successfully into a corporation if employees are smart enough to understand it and understand it quickly. Entrepreneurs of smaller businesses should place more emphasis on employee training on a regular basis. They should encourage their employees to take advantage of inexpensive training courses offered by public organizations. By so doing, they can realize technological sophistication step by step.

Chapter 4
PRODUCTION MANAGEMENT AND THE WORKER

At the initial stage of development, production management primarily meant the management of workers. However, automation and computerization have changed the worker's role in the field of production, thereby changing the nature of production management. In this chapter, changes in production and pre-production arrangements are delineated.

4.1 CHANGING DEMOGRAPHY

As discussed in the previous chapter, automation and computerization change the production system and its management. In this chapter, the impact of automation and computerization is viewed from the standpoint of workers.

The worker is an indispensable component of the corporation. On the other hand, the worker population is part of the working environment of the corporation. The expression "internal environment" is used in the latter sense. Simply stated, the worker is an employee of the corporation and at the same time a member of the community to which the corporation belongs. The employee's behaviour within the corporate framework is determined by his values as a community member. Such values evolve as years go by, influencing the worker's motivation and attitude towards work. The corporation should formulate its production system and management to suit the changing values of the employees.

The ways in which people participate in production has changed. In the first place, people are becoming better educated. In Japan, the percentage of primary school graduates advancing to junior high school in 1940 is comparable to the percentage of high school graduates entering into colleges and universities today. With today's workers better educated than workers of forty years ago, it is not rare to find college graduates operating machines in factories. Possessing more education, workers expect more mental satisfaction. College graduates may obtain such satisfaction by doing programming or maintenance for machining centres rather than performing repetitive work on an assembly line. In other words, the production system and its management should change as workers receive higher education.

Second, there are numerous part-timers, mostly women, working in offices and factories in Japan. It is important to provide these workers with a pleasant working environment where simple jobs can be made more interesting and part-timers can be involved in small group activities. Proper designing and administration of production systems should be reinforced by enthusiastic participation of part-timers in day-to-day work. This type of production management improves productivity.

In a certain factory producing precision plastic moldings, female part-timers on the assembly line contributed in large measure to the vitalization of the working environment through their small group activities. They discussed work improvements and came up with creative suggestions for regular workers in the work station up stream. It is wrong to assume that part-timers are outside the framework of production management.

Third, there is the aging of workers as they pass the retirement age of fifty-five. The age of retirement has been moved upwards worldwide. Very soon, Japanese corporations may change their policies and retain their workers until the age of sixty. As early as the 1960s, the age of sixty-five was generally accepted in the United States as the retirement age for blue-collar workers. Healthy workers are fully capable of and entitled to serve the community up to the age of seventy. They can make contributions by sharing their experience with others as well as working themselves.

It is desirable to have mature workers as field leaders to formulate targets for each working group. They encourage the group to contribute fully towards better production management through their guidance. This is the human aspect of production management. The author is acquainted with one small firm and another medium-sized firm in Japan which successfully implemented this idea.

Fourth, there is an increase in the number of inhouse specialists. As the number of manufacturing units increases and pre-production arrangements become more complex, the corporate work force must have specialists in production techniques, design, research and development, and administration. For instance, one fourth of the workforce of Boeing Aircraft Company, the world's largest producer of commercial aircraft, is said to consist of skilled technicians, engineers, and scientists as of 1980. Technology-oriented corporations maintain a large pool of specialists.

Production management, in the broad sense, includes the management of these specialists. Since specialists are engaged in sophisticated and complex work, management by outsiders would not succeed. Training in work management is recommended for the specialists to let them manage themselves. This type of self-management should always be growth-oriented.

The production system should be able to respond to the expectations of the four different working groups discussed above. Production management should motivate and encourage the growth of workers. Thorough comprehension of these points leads a corporation to success.

4.2 CHANGE IN THE ROLE OF WORKERS

The less developed the machine is, the more important is the worker's skill. The operator of an old type lathe must be a skilled worker. Here, the human factor is more important than the machine factor. The rapid industrial advancement in the United States, in the past few decades, created a shortage in the supply of skilled workers. The Ford-type assembly line which utilizes a large number of unskilled labour was initiated just at this time. Such human sea tactics were humiliating to workers. Although the Ford-type assembly line realized high productivity due to its excellent production engineering structure, it failed to give due consideration to workers as human beings. The workers lost interest in their work because the jobs they were assigned were invariably too monotonous. The proverbial empty Coke can sealed inside the door of an American made car eloquently dipicts the state of mind of disenchanted workers.

The significance of this human element was established by the famous Hawthorne experiments in the last half of the 1920s. Various experiments were subsequently conducted on the significance of workers' morale in the workplace. Those experiments proved that female workers are better suited for simple repetitive work than are male workers. Young workers are better suited than older workers. Young workers tolerate repetitive work because they can look to the future in terms of promotion whereas older workers become disenchanted. These experiments did not provide a solution to the fundamental problem of treating workers as human beings. The solution for assembly type work came from automation. A large number of automated assembly machines are already in use in the electronics industry. Technological advancements in electronics have made automated assembly work economically viable. Although this cannot apply to all kinds of complicated assembly work, the emancipation of human beings from simple repetitive work is taking place at an accelerated pace during the 1980s.

There still exist many assembly lines basically dependent on repetitive human labour. How did Japanese manufacturing establishments succeed in motivating workers on these assembly line? The Japanese automobile industry adopted a job rotation system to keep workers interested in their work. Workers would change their work stations several times a day to relieve boredom. This system, called horizontal job enlargement, boosts the worker's performance capability because he has to do several jobs a day instead of one.

The Japanese automobile industry also trained its workers for preventive maintenance and simple repair jobs. This is another type of job sophistication in the field which is called vertical job enlargement.

The third scheme adopted by the Japanese automobile industry was that of organizing small group activities in conjunction with suggestion systems. Several field workers form a group and from regular discussions find suggestions for improving their daily job performance. This is a type of autonomous work management which is basically foreign to conventional management methodologies. Such autonomous work management is a product of horizontal work enlargement.

Furthermore, self-disciplinary scheduling and inventory control, called the Toyota "Kan-ban" system was implemented on each field group consisting of about 50 to 60 workers. Other types of self-disciplinary control are being implemented in the United States. All of these motivation-oriented schemes have one thing in common, an appreciation of the worker's initiative. Needles to say, education and on-the-job training, prior to the implementation of such schemes are indispensable.

Production management is implemented by delegating authority to field workers. Quality, work (both labour and machine), time, quantity, and cost are controlled primarily in the field. The problem is in coordinating such controls in the field with the management function of plant manager, division manager, and president. The answer lies in the creation of a clear-cut production management flow involving the entire corporate organization with emphasis on autonomous control in the field. Field workers are once again masters of the machine because they can control it through modification or incorporation of their own ideas. They make the decisions on operating the machine and on modifying it. Figure 4-1 shows the historical evolution of the workers' role in production activities.

4.3 PRODUCTION MANAGEMENT AND THE SOCIOTECHNICAL APPROACH

What is stated in the previous section is similar to the sociotechnical approach of the Tavistock Institute of Human Relations of the United Kingdom. The research on coal mines done by this institute is known throughout the world. This institute maintains that technological advancement does not always work well for the worker. Therefore, the adjustment

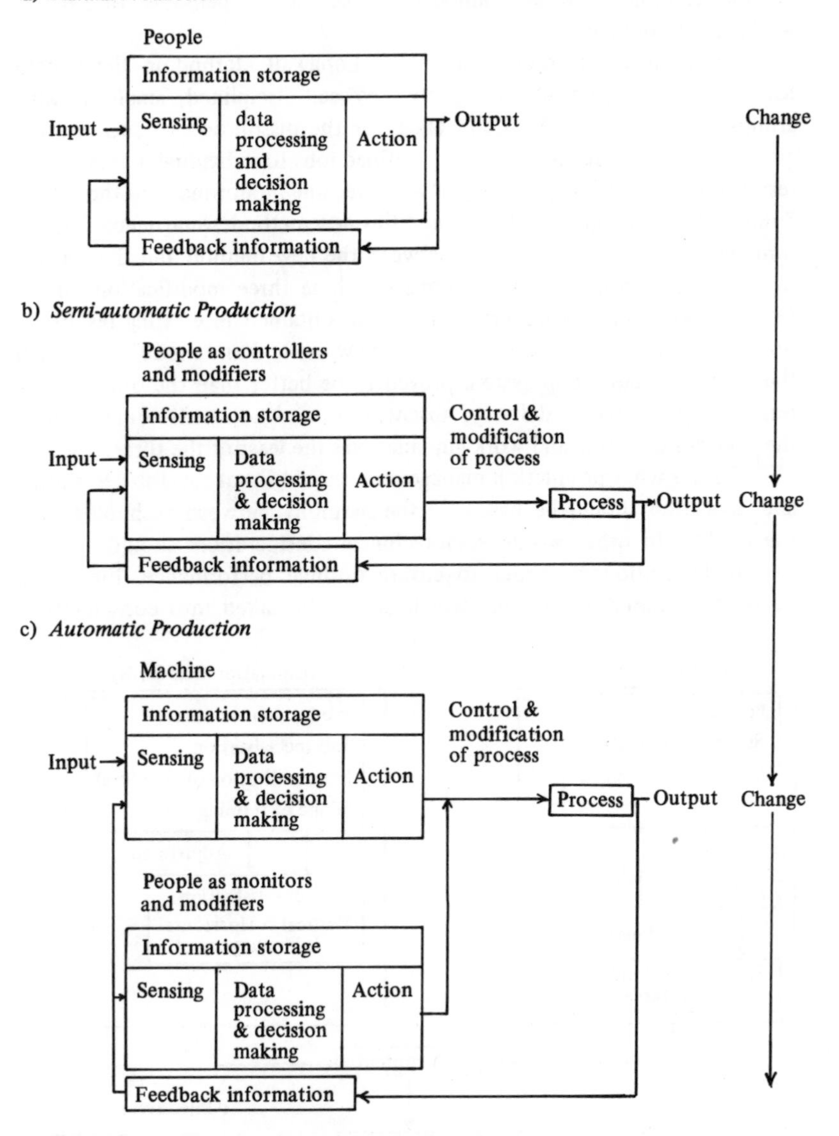

Figure 4-1 Workers' Role in Production Activity

Source: Elwood S. Buffa, *Operations Management: The Management of Production Systems*, John Wiley, 1976. p. 271, with some modifications on b) and c) relative to the role of people as modifiers of production process.

of new technologies to accommodate workers is indispensable for a better working environment.

Prior to the introduction of the Longwall Method in the United Kingdom, excavation was conducted by self-disciplined, small working groups. The Longwall Method called for the dissolution of such worker groups and the allocation of rigidly defined jobs to individual workers. As a result, output was boosted but the work became monotonous to the miner. Some British coal mines fully adopted this new method, some rejected it, and some worked out a compromise between the new method and the conventional worker group method. Comparing these three modifications of the Longwall Method, researchers at Tavistosk obtained interesting results. In brief, those mines which introduced the new method and modified it to suit the existing small group system proved to be better than the other two in terms of productivity, delivery, absenteeism, and accidents. Furthermore, the need for overtime and work guidance was the least of the three.

This is what production management should shoot for. Job description and allocation should be based on the harmony between technology and the worker. In other words, sociotechnical considerations should be given to job descriptions in order to ensure optimal performance. Figure 4-2 shows the related parameters which should be taken into consideration.

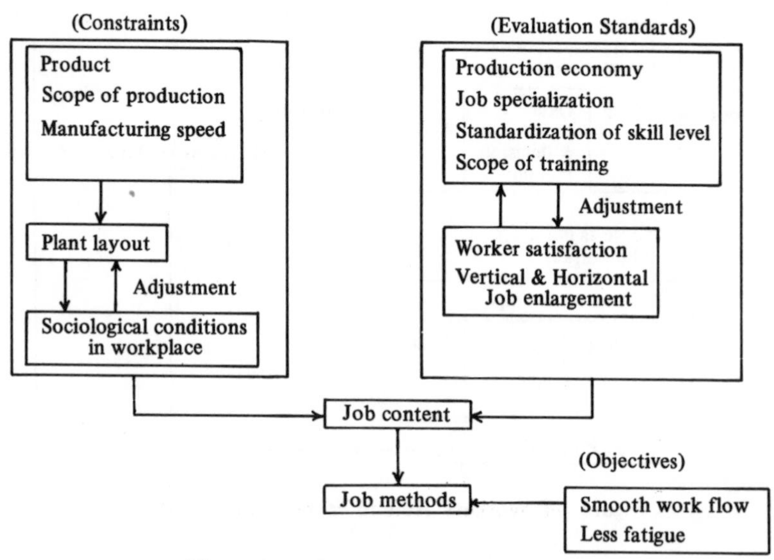

Figure 4-2 Sociotechnical Job Designing

Note: The figure in Elwood S. Buffa, op. cit., p. 261 was modified to suit the subject of this book.

The importance of worker satisfaction should not endanger the existence of a corporation due to loss of competitiveness. This is where work specialization comes in. Industrial engineers would argue in favour of equalization in the skill level of workers assigned to identical jobs as it simplifies work scheduling and control. Traditionally, employers try to break down manufacturing processes into small job segments to make the best use of cheap unskilled labour. Contrary to this, there are employers who encourage vertical as well as horizontal job enlargement on the part of workers. Job satisfaction is then obtainable through learning and voluntary work improvement.

Figure 4-2 lists human constraints and those related to production techniques. Product design and the scope of production are determined primarily by requirements in the market independent of the workers' desires. Manufacturing speed is chiefly a function of competition. In plant layout and production processes, optimization should be accomplished in sociological as well as technoeconomic factors. Before plant relocation, in Japan, the management invariably asks employees' opinions on the equipment layout and the production process designs for the new facility. A common practice is to centrally locate a space for workers' relaxation and thus create personal pride in the new plant, a driving force in worker motivation and productivity improvement.

As discussed so far, it is a difficult task to design and implement field work using the sociotechnological approach. There invariably is a wide gap between the organization's drive for continuous cost reduction and the desire to maximize satisfaction on the part of the worker. Figure 4-3 shows that what the worker would do to maximize satisfaction is by nature very much different from what he is expected to do to minimize production cost. The discrepancy between the two should be eliminated through compromise on the part of the management and aggressive work improvement on the part of the worker. The sociotechnical approach to production management emphasizes job designing which in a sense is a type of pre-production arrangement.

4.4 PRE-PRODUCTION ARRANGEMENTS AND PRODUCTION MANAGEMENT

In this section some points are discussed that relate the management of people who are engaged in pre-production arrangements to product planning and design, research and development.

When viewed from the standpoint of the corporate organization, pre-production arrangements encompass the production engineering department (preparation for production), the technical department (product planning and designing), and the research and development

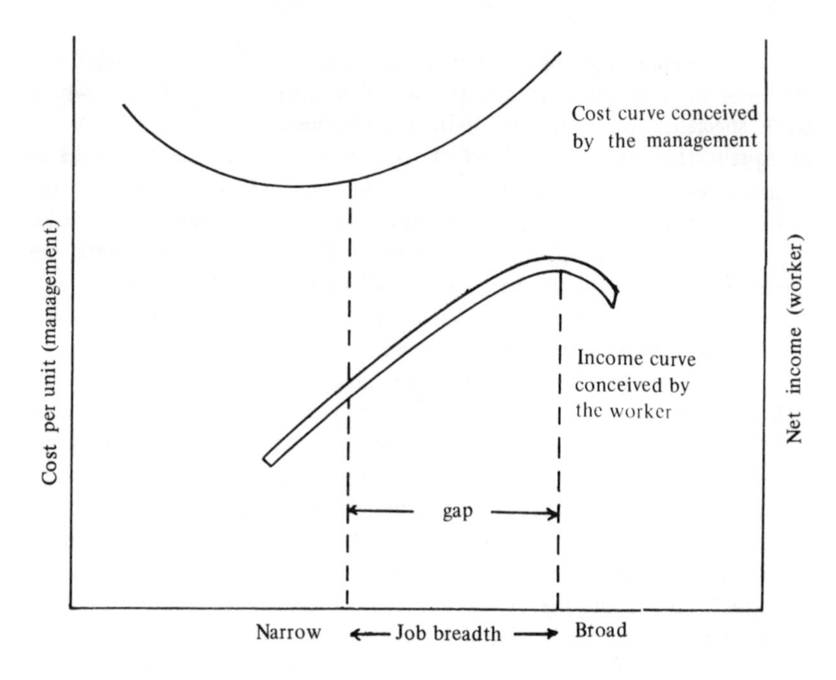

Figure 4-3 Job Expectation Management vs. Worker

Note: The two graphs in Elwood S. Buffa, op. cit., pp. 259–260 are referred.

department. People in such departments are specialized technicians, engineers and scientists with the exception of a small number of administrative managers and staffs. The further technology advances, the more human resources are allocated to pre-production arrangements, particularly in the case of large corporations.

Efficient management of pre-production arrangements is possible only through systematically classifying the work related to it. Efficiency further requires that pre-production period be shortened in order to enhance sensitivity towards developments in the market. This subject will be discussed in detail in Section 6-4 in Chapter 6.

Design group technology is a recent attempt to classify design activities in production-related jobs. This technology is geared to avoid unnecessary design complications and to consolidate similar functions into one communal design and work process. For instance, in the case of drilling, plates in different shapes and sizes may be processed in one lot if the plate material and the thickness are uniform. Plate material should be standardized as much as possible. Such standardization in parts design gave rise to partial automation, resulting in automatic drafting machines and computer aided design, called CAD. However, the generation of creative ideas and designs still belongs in the human domain.

All pre-production arrangements including product planning and design, and R & D are heavily dependent on computers for information gathering and analysis. This paves the way for eventual automation and standardization of the work through computer-based data accumulation. Brain and manual work are gradually being taken over by the tripartite brain-machine-computer combination.

What is the key to production management of pre-production arrangements? The key is self-disciplinary management in the field. Let us cite an example.

Hewlett Packard, one of the largest manufacturers of electronics equipment in American and the world, owes three-quarters of its sales to products developed during the past five years. At Hewlett Packard, products are developed by teams of four to fifteen researchers. Team members conduct market surveys, set up research objectives, and work out budgets and schedules on their own. Internal team meetings are held at least once a month for coordination and evaluation purposes. In this manner, the team members enthusiastically carry out the work, considering the project their "baby".

Instructions from above are kept to a bare minimum. An employee can manage his own work as long as he observes basic corporate philosophies stated in clear cut language covering profit, customers, product development, growth, employees, business administration, and corporate responsibility towards the community. In reference to business administration policy, freedom of action and an appropriately defined objective should be given to each employee so that objectives are realized in a positive and creative manner. The Hewlett Packard philosophy emphasizes the importance of free thinking for the generation of innovative ideas. This is a valuable suggestion to those who are interested in production management.

4.5 WORKERS IN SMALL AND MEDIUM-SIZED FIRMS

Let us briefly discuss some people-oriented production management issues peculiar to small and medium-sized firms.

Typically, a higher percentage of their work force consists of part-timers and aged workers compared with larger corporations. Their production systems and work layouts are relatively simple. Therefore, production management should be simple. Self-management by workers in the field is not immediately feasible with the considerable degree of education and training required beforehand.

There are also fewer specialists in pre-production stages compared with larger corporations. As a result, production management is synonymous with manufacturing control, and work control is synonymous with production work control. Automation and computerization are not as advanced as in larger corporations and assembly lines are primarily based on human labour. Under such circumstances, the emphasis should be placed on long-term education and training of employees to give them the motivation to improve themselves by their own initiative.

The first pre-requisite for introducing mechatronics is the workers' willingness and capability to implement it. Successful introduction of new technologies means a lot more than the installation of state-of-the-art equipment. Constant worker education and training direct the manufacturing organization towards new technologies and automation. Therefore, the primary objective of production management for small and medium-sized firms should be to nurture workers' initiatives.

Chapter 5
STRATEGY, ORGANIZATION, AND PRODUCTION MANAGEMENT

Production management is closely related to corporate strategy and organization. It is important to clarify that corporate strategies centred around specialization, diversification, and integration are realized through production management. This chapter discusses manufacturing organizations that are categorized according to their size and pre-production arrangements.

5.1 STRATEGIES AND THE PRODUCTION PROCESS

What is corporate strategy? Generally, it is defined as the process and result of decision making on the part of the corporate management in finding the direction the business should follow in relation to its environment. A typical example is the evolution of new businesses. New businesses are motivated either by technological advancement or developments in the market. Let us analyze how ideas are transformed into new businesses.

If the new idea is not based on a new technology, a market survey is conducted to determine the feasibility of developing the idea into a new business. If the new idea is based on a new technology, forecasting and assessment of the technology is conducted in addition to a market survey. In this case, the corporate strategy is influenced by technology forecasting, a market survey, and technology assessment. Results of these pre-production activities are used as the initial input for strategy implementation.

If the decision is made to form a new business, the first item of investment requiring definition is research and development. Research and development strategy is formulated at this stage. Step-by-step evaluation is made throughout the cycle to determine the feasibility of proceeding to the next step. If feasibility is established a decision has to be made according to the corporate strategy on product planning and designing.

Next comes a variety of activities for the inauguration of commercial production which are called "pre-production arrangements" in this book. In the preliminary steps of production, a well-organized implementation programme is required for site selection, conceptual plant layout, plant design, production flow including sub-contractors, equipment installation, equipment selection, people mobilization including training, utility supply, and material purchasing. Such a programme should be in conformity with the corporate strategy. The activities are collectively called a project which is a type of production activity requiring a special project type management.

Upon completion of all the aforementioned activity, pilot production begins followed by-full scale production. To what extent are these activities based on corporate strategy? The answer is "the extent to which top management is involved in decision making."

Research and development programmes requiring substantial budget allocations and extended periods of implementation are directly based on corporate strategy. Research and development programmes of such a magnitude are not rare in the case of large corporations. The chief executive officer of a large Japanese manufacturer said recently that product development efforts lasting 100 years were not unusual for initiation of major new businesses.

Production of new products (the inauguration of mass production on a commercial basis) is also directly dependent on the corporate strategy. Judging from the scope of impact both in time and money, the decisions on location, quantity, and scope of internal as well as external production should all be governed by the corporate strategy. Is the production plant going to be located in the country or somewhere overseas (siting strategy)? What should be the initial production capacity (plant construction strategy)? To what extent should suppliers be used (equipment investment and material flow strategies)? These are questions requiring answers by top management.

How does the corporate strategy affect production activity itself? In a new business, the annual production programme or target for normal operations should be based on the corporate strategy. The determination of production quantity is based on developments in the market. The corporate strategy provides a target for production management. The corporate strategy also provides targets for research and development, product planning, product design, and pre-production arrangements. Figure 5-1 shows this relationship in connection with technology forecasting, market surveys, and technology assessment.

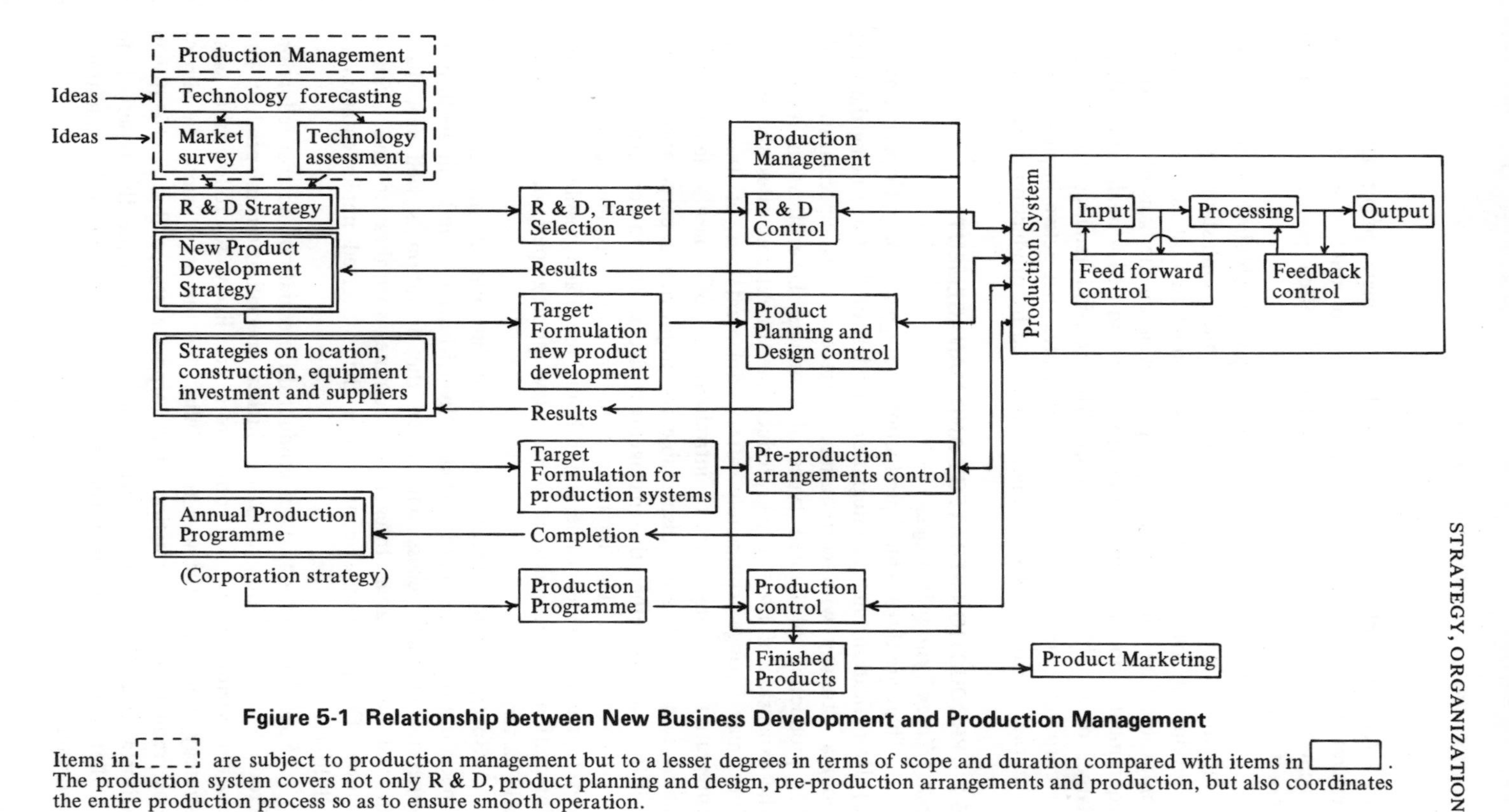

Fgiure 5-1 Relationship between New Business Development and Production Management

Items in [dashed box] are subject to production management but to a lesser degrees in terms of scope and duration compared with items in [solid box]. The production system covers not only R & D, product planning and design, pre-production arrangements and production, but also coordinates the entire production process so as to ensure smooth operation.

As previously mentioned, production management aims at the realization of production goals. However, if production goals cannot be reached, those goals have to be changed, often resulting in strategy modifications.

Suppose quality, time, and cost targets, established on the basis of competition in the market call for too much sophistication, too short a production period and too low a production cost, all of which are impossible from the standpoint of production on the basis of the existing equipment. Should machining centres be introduced to realize the original target or should production stop? The decision requires consideration in corporate strategy. This example indicates that active implementation of corporate strategies sometimes is triggered by production management.

5.2 PRODUCTION STRATEGY AND MANAGEMENT

5.2.1 Three Typical Strategies

There are three typical production strategies, namely, 1) specialization, 2) diversification, and 3) integration, the last of the three being the most popular strategy with corporations in recent years. Specialization calls for production of limited types of products. Diversification results in the expansion of the existing product line. In extreme cases, the product line may change completely after implementation of this strategy. Integration means the introduction of new technological innovations which are indispensable for improving a corporation's competitive edge, whether the management decides to go for specialization or diversification. The importance of integration is illustrated by the development of video cameras for home use made possible through the integration of technologies in circuitry, photography, data processing, and battery.

Specialization, diversification and integration are inter-related. Specialization sometimes needs diversification and diversification generates competitiveness only when the operation is well specialized in each product area. Integration promotes specialization and diversification. Competitiveness comes from the concerted implementation of all three.

Specialization consists of product differentiation and cost reduction. Product differentiation calls for higher specialization in product and market segmentation. As competitors are likely to follow the same strategy, this is not the way to stability. On the other hand, the aim of cost reduction is the creation of a corporate stance that is effective in withstanding the type of price competition frequently observed in markets for mature products such as textiles, veneer lumber, and traditional ceramics.

Cost reduction is applicable to every stage of production and sales activity. Direct distribution, production scale enlargement through specialization, simplification of the production process, extensive use of part timers, materials improvement through advanced technology, production yield improvement, and extensive use of external suppliers are among such cost reduction efforts. The most efficient specialization can be expected from a proper mixing of product differentiation and cost reduction. Corporations will be successful even in a mature market if they can supply quality product at a good price.

Diversification strategies are of three forms: 1) existing technology-related, 2) existing market-related, and 3) no relation at all either to existing technology or markets.

1) In the first type of diversification strategy, new products are created and marketed making use of technological expertise accumulated in-house. This route is frequently taken by electric home appliance manufacturers.
2) The second methodology calls for the introduction of new products to markets already secured by the manufacturer. Dunhill of the United Kingdom is a good example. Recently, in order to recover from poor sales performance, Dunhill introduced men's apparel and office- and travel-related products to cater to high income clientele long nurtured for its smoking articles.
3) Diversification unrelated to accumulated technology or existing markets can be accomplished in a variety of different ways. This route includes tie-ups with other corporations on production and distribution, either permanent or temporary in nature. Whatever the deployment format, the objective is to reinforce specialization and diversification.

5.2.2 Relationship between Production Strategy and Management

What impact does strategy deployment have on production management? The strategies of specialization and differentiation result in smaller production lots for a large variety of products complicating production management. On the other hand, the cost reduction strategy aims at a simplified production management through simplification of the production system. In the case of mixed deployment of differentiation and cost reduction, one of the most basic and important strategies in manufacturing industry, a unique production system of complex structure should be covered by a simple production management scheme. This is a challenge for production management today.

How does diversification affect production management? Technology-related diversification should not require drastic modification of production management due to similarity in the production system. However, market related diversification is quite different. In the Dunhill case, for instance, the production of men's apparel, office-, and travel-related goods is a new experience requiring the study of related production management. When Dunhill first decided to produce stationery, the management introduced related technologies and know-how from Mont Blanc of West Germany. But that was not enough. Dunhill ended up taking over Mont Blanc to secure technological competiveness in stationery. This development verifies the importance of technology and expertise in the production system and its management.

As discussed in the first section of this chapter, diversification related neither to technology nor market is change-oriented

The last of the three types of strategy is integration If the integration process constitutes a non-repetitive project by itself, it is considered to be a type of single-unit production compatible with project-type production management. If such integration includes a joint venture extending over a long period of time, its production system and management should be based on a consensus among the participating corporations. If the venture is international, each participating corporation should have a well-structured, written manual on its production system and management in order to avoid unnecessary misunderstanding during the joint-venture undertaking.

5.3 PRODUCTION ORGANIZATION AND MANAGEMENT

Unlike the preceding abstract discussion, this section examines actual organizations in production plants.

5.3.1 Structural Hierarchy in the Field

It is said the field force, made up of workers in the production section, has influence over the management in Japanese manufacturing corporations. In large Japanese corporations, the production section encompasses three structural tiers of "Kakari", "Kumi" and "Han". World-renowned Quality Circles (QC) belong to the "Han" level. Several field workers join together to form a QC group, with an experienced member as the leader. Although informal, the QC group is the basic unit of organization in substance. Two or three QC groups join together to form a "Han" with their leader called a "Han-cho". Two or three "Han"s make a "Kumi" with a "Kumi-cho" as the leader. Proceeding up the heirarchy, "Kakari" and section ("Ka") are similarly structured. See Figure 5.2.

One production section can easily comprise more than 100 people, a rare phenomenon for smaller corporations. Unit leaders in each hierarchical

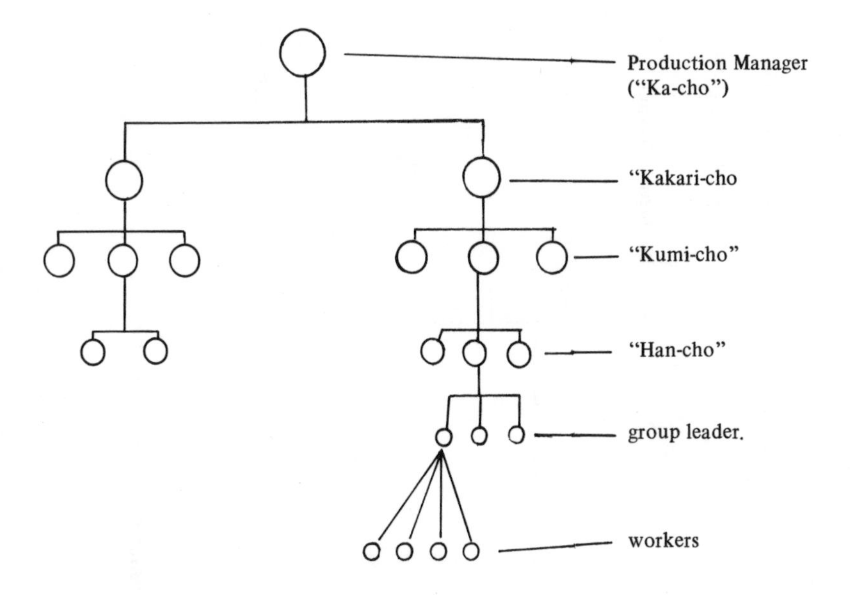

Figure 5-2 Production Organization Hierarchy

Each unit consists of a few units belonging to one tier below in the hierarchy. For instance, a "Han" consists of two to three group leaders and each group leader heads a group comprising three to five workers.

tier are appointed through promotion based on competence and experience. Many production "Ka-cho"s who started from the bottom tier are respected by field workers. College graduates would be stranded without the cooperation of field leaders.

Within the framework of a production plant, in addition to the production section, there normally are other sections for scheduling control, quality control, maintenance, production engineering, and general affairs. Work, inventory, and cost control is under the jurisdiction of the production section. The plant manager and the deputy plant manager are above section chiefs or "Kacho"s.

5.3.2 Inter-federally Decentralized Unit

One product division normally consists of a few plants and several administrative departments that manage purchasing, sales, production planning, and quality control. In some cases, the administrative departments are responsible for product planning and design. (See Figure 5-3).

Within the divisional framework, the production section with

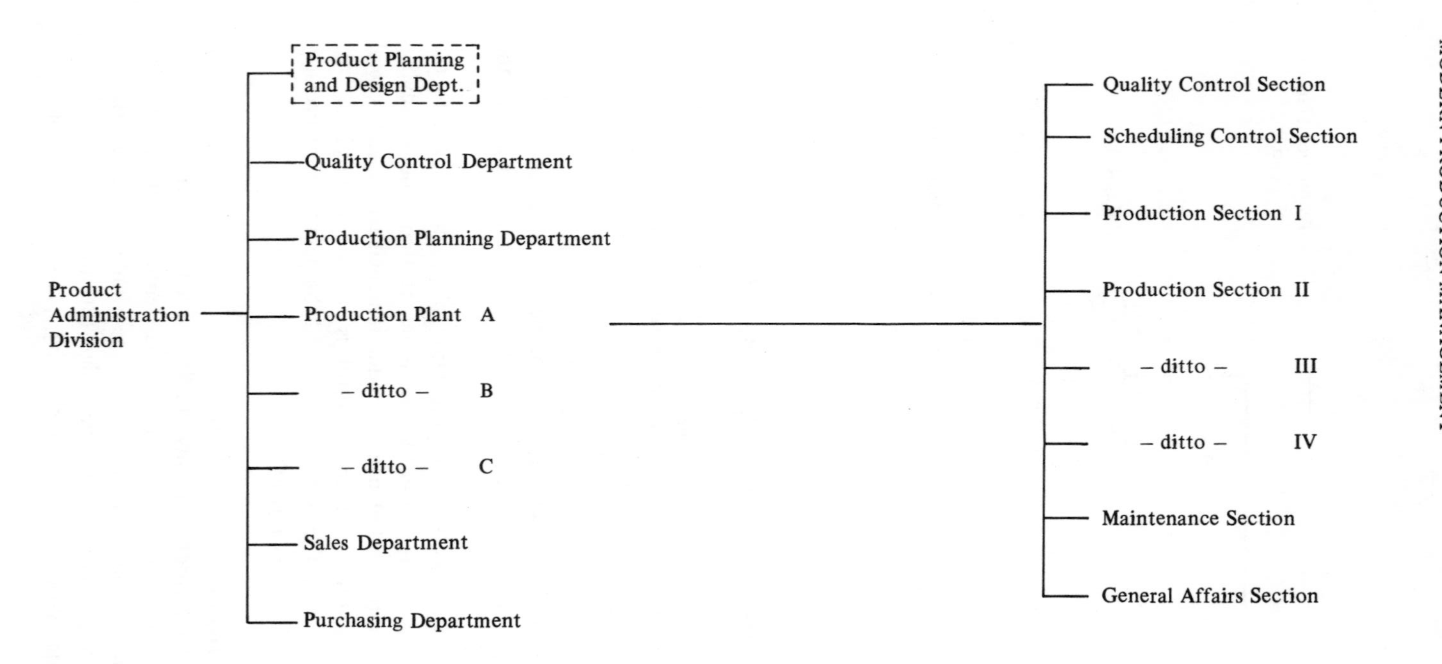

Figure 5-3 Typical Organization of a Product Administration Division

Note: The Product Planning and Design Department may belong to the headquarters.

assistance from the scheduling and quality control sections is responsible for implementation. The corporate headquarters is responsible for coordinating changes in marketing, corporate strategy and the business environment.

5.3.3 Organization for Pre-production Arrangements

The production engineering division is responsible for pre-production arrangements, with the possible exception of product planning and design. If not performed by this division, it must be executed by the engineering or the design department at the headquarters. Either the research department or the laboratory is responsible for R & D. For certain corporations, R & D responsibilities are shared by divisions and the headquarters. Time saving has become a critical factor for pre-production arrangements in recent years. Production management is geared to the shortening of time requiring for pre-production arrangements, product planning and design without adversely affecting product cost, product quality, or moral among employees.

As stated before, guidelines for production management are generated by the headquarters. For instance, the target for production cost is finalized by the headquarters and given to the production plants. Specialists at the headquarters on training and worker mobilization participate in the formulation of targets for personnal management.There is a planning group on a permanent basis which acts as the secretariat for coordinating production management and marketing, corporate strategy for new products and businesses, and modification of the production system due to a changing environment.

The final decision making body for technology forecasting, market surveys and technology assessment is normally a top management committee assisted by the planning group. This committee may invite outside experts from time to time, or may appoint a task force on a temporary basis. All other strategy-related matters are handled by the planning group at the headquarters. Such responsibility sharing and participation are indicated in Figure 5-4.

5.3.4 Organization Format and Production Management

Production-oriented organizations may be categorized into 1) function-oriented organizations, 2) project-oriented organizations, 3) product-based organizations, 4) matrix organizations, and 5) venture-oriented organizations.

Function-oriented organization: An organization structure based on work steps. In this case, production management is also implemented on the basis of work steps.

	Headquarters	Product Administration Divisions	Manufacturing Plants
Technology forecasting	O		
Market surveys	O		
Technology assessment	O		
Research and Development	O	O	
Product Planning and Design	O	O	
Pre-production arrangements	O	O	O
Production	O	O	O
Marketing	O	O	

Figure 5-4 Functional Responsibility Sharing

Note: Authority should be delegated to divisions and plants as much as possible.

Project-oriented organization: An organization of an ad hoc nature formulated to complete a project. In this case, production management is implemented on an individual project basis.

Product-based organization: Either an integration of process-based organizations or multi-functional organizations capable of completing an entire production process for a limited number of products. Production management is also implemented on a product basis.

Matrix organization: A relatively new type of organization where project management is implemented horizontally across functional organizations. In most cases the project management is product based, but sometimes cost reduction or quality control is taken as the management parameter. Production management is complex in this case, because the responsibility for personnel management goes to the head of the functional group while project completion is under the jurisdiction of the project manager. Since this type of organization is becoming increasingly popular for innovative or highly sophisticated projects, effective methodologies need to be devised to implement production management smoothly. When projects are designed to reduce production cost the project manager is involved in production activity on a daily basis. Production management of routine activities should be implemented in parallel with the management of change. This is possible only through the enthusiastic participation of the project manager as well as the field work force. See Figure 5-5.

Venture-oriented organization: An independent organization within the corporate structure vested with authority to perform a new business. It is just like a company within a company. The manager of such an organization can be compared to the president of a smaller corporation. As in the case of smaller corporations, production management is not implemented in a specialized manner. Attention should be focussed on pre-production management.

5.4 STRATEGIES AND ORGANIZATIONS FOR SMALLER CORPORATIONS

The specialization strategy is more suitable for smaller corporations than large corporations. Efficiency is enhanced when the strategy is a mixture of differentiation and cost reduction. However, this means a complex production system and a complex management. Production and management techniques need improvement. Here, the integration strategy should be considered by the management of smaller corporations.

In a small manufacturing firm with ten employees, the proprietor is the sole manager. If the business grows, there will be more employees, and the proprietor will need an assistant to manage people so that he can allocate more time to customer calls and financial matters. As the firm grows even larger, the proprietor appoints a few field managers to delegate part of his authority on personnel management. But production management has not been established as an independent function because the field manager's authority is limited primarily to conformance with the work schedule, reduction of defects, and motivation of employees, while all major items are within the purview of the proprietor.

The establishment of production control as a separate function may be possible if there are more than fifty employees in a corporation. A corporation with more than 100 employees would find it difficult to do without a production manager. As the corporate organization grows larger, schedule management, quality control, and maintenance will be handled by different managers or sections.

		Production Section				
		I	II	III	IV	V
Project	A	*	*	*	*	*
	B	*	*	*	*	*
	C	*	*	*	*	*
	D	*	*	*	*	*

*shows that there are two bosses in each section. The one is a project manager, and the other is a section head.

Figure 5-5 A Tvpical Matrix Organization

Figure 5-6 shows a typical organization in this case. The scheduling control section is independent from the quality control section in view of the importance of these two functions to production. The plant manager and line managers are responsible for education, training, and motivation of employees. Equipment maintenance is a separate function which evolves into plant engineering in larger corporations. The control of work, quantity, cost, profit, other specific items, and pre-production arrangements is performed by the proprietor himself with the help of the plant manager and line managers on an ad hoc basis.

Engineering in Figure 5-6 infers the designing of products or parts, an important function for smaller manufacturing firms. Research and development in smaller firms is usually not a full-time job. R & D on a limited scale might be conducted by employees who also help with product design, pre-production arrangements, and equipment maintenance from time to time. The proprietor himself may serve as the R & D specialist if the budget is really small. Each person has to wear more than one hat when so few cover a full range of production management activities.

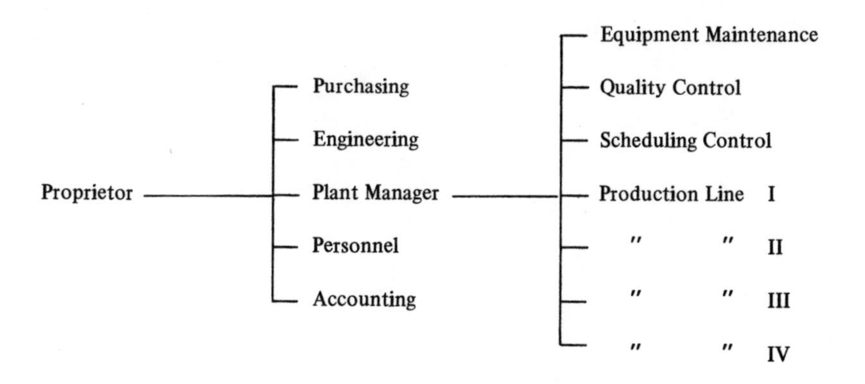

Figure 5-6 Typical Organization of Smaller Manufacturing Firms

PART TWO

DEPLOYMENT OF PRODUCTION MANAGEMENT

Chapter 6

DEMAND FLUCTUATION AND PRODUCTION MANAGEMENT

Production management has to eventually respond to demand in the market. This chapter deals with the four representative types of production management: 1) production management geared to reduce production cost, 2) production management to implement multi-variety small lot production, 3) production management to shorten and sustain production lead time and, 4) production management to maintain high quality and low price.

6.1 CHANGING NEEDS

How will a change in demand affect production management? There will be severe competition throughout the 1980s. There is unlikely to be a recurrence of the rapid economic growth that took place in Japan in the first half of the 1970s. The growth rate in the market as a whole will probably go down, resulting in tougher competition for corporations.

6.1.1 Increasing Competition

The correct way to cope with tough competition is to develop a new market or to enhance one's share of an existing market through the introduction of new products. In actual practice, however, there is a considerable amount of risk involved in this methodology. A surer way is cost reduction. The problem with cost reduction is that it is not a one-time affair because competitors also try to reduce their production cost. In the future, many corporations will choose production management as the means of achieving cost reduction.

6.1.2 Changing Consumer Taste

Customers' tastes also change. The types of high quality textile products which enjoyed brisk demand immediately after World War II are no longer popular even among the comparatively low-income consumers in the 1980s. Unless you are creating works of art, you cannot afford to keep on producing the same goods for ten years. One must be alert to changes in consumers' tastes to keep production facilities from becoming obsolete.

Large textile manufacturers are shifting their emphasis from textile materials to finished products because their survival depends on how well they can respond to changing consumer needs in finished products. Such a shift will mean drastic changes in the production system and production management.

6.1.3 Diversification in Demand

Consumers' needs have been diversified. Needs are diversified even for the same type of product. For instance, there is a vast variety of television sets. Some TV sets have very large screens while small ones are built into watches. The market has been well segmented, and manufacturers are striving to maintain supremacy of their brand image over that of competitors.

As discussed in chapter 5, the specialization strategy, a hybrid of differentiation and cost reduction, is compatible with market segmentation. In most cases, differentiation results, in smaller production lots, making it harder to reduce production cost. As a part of the corporate strategy of small scale production of a large variety of products, production management should be implemented efficiently to reduce production cost.

6.1.4 Shorter Product Life

Product life in the market is becoming increasingly shorter. Ready-made apparel has a very short product life because demand changes for each season. Producers are lucky if they can begin production only after confirming demand. In the case of high quality ready-to-wear apparel, they make a limited number and watch sales before deciding to make a few more. In this case, there is close coordination between production and sales. With the production period so short, delivery must be quick. Again, production management is the key.

6.1.5 Delivery Reliability

Once delivery dates are set, they must be adhered to. Shorter lead time and lower price cannot be used as an excuse for late delivery. This is particularly true in the case of subcontractors delivering parts to large manufacturers. These suppliers cannot afford to produce parts on estimation in order to avoid late deliveries because an unnecessarily large inventory could make them unfit for survival. A production system should be structured to accommodate quick and reliable deliveries in order to win the trust of customers. According to a survey by the author, unreliable delivery is the most serious difficulty for industries in developing countries. Other specialists agree with this observation. Precise scheduling control is often a source of competitiveness, particularly for firms supplying parts and components to large manufacturers.

6.1.6 High Quality and Low Price

Reliable delivery is of little importance if a product is rejected by the customer. Cost reduction should not adversely affect the delivery period or product quality. Sometimes, product quality needs to be improved without affecting the price or delivery period. Customers are becoming increasingly demanding of quality. It is not easy to respond to such customer needs without adversely affecting other parameters. Through rigorous utilization of advanced technologies and value analysis (V.A.), new materials or mechanics must be found which are capable of performing the same function at a lower price. Quality control should be an integrated control of quality, covering not only production but also pre-production arrangements.

The following sections of this chapter analyze production management from the standpoint of sales. Production cannot exist without sales. Therefore, good production management should aim at eventual success in the market.

First, cost-reduction-oriented production management will be discussed. Second is industrial dynamics and demand-pull production discussed as a production management methodology designed to cope with small scale production of a large variety of products, a common prescription for both diversified customer needs and short product life. Third, time control methodologies are examined as a mean of realizing short delivery period. Particular attention will be drawn to PERT (Programme Evaluation and Review Technique) which is a suitable methodology for project management of R & D, product planning and design, preparation for production, and production and sales. Last, quality control in response to needs in the market will be discussed briefly.

6.2 COST REDUCTION-ORIENTED PRODUCTION MANAGEMENT

In actual practice, production management should include the management of production, pre-production arrangements, product planning, design, and research and development. Cost reduction efforts should be based on an analysis of production cost and the R & D budget, including personnel expenses and general administrative expenses. This means the reduction of total expense incurred by all concerned departments or sections. The parameters used for analyzing production are materials costs, payments to suppliers, wages, depreciation, and indirect cost.

6.2.1 Reduction in Materials Costs and Payments to Suppliers

Material selection through VA activities brings about a reduction in material costs. Inexpensive material or mechanics may be used without changing the performance of the product. Substitution is made possible through exhaustive R & D efforts. The implementation process may include a drastic change in the production process. A trade-off should always be considered between the saving in material cost and the expense of implementing a VA activity.

Yield improvement is important to materials cost reduction. The rejection rate is reduced through feed forward control, a pre-feeding check on materials related to quality control. Workers should be instructed and motivated to perform their jobs carefully (feed forward control). Work results are evaluated on a daily basis in terms of rejection rates to emphasize quality consciousness among workers (feedback control). These measures improve yields through work control.

Yields may be improved through modification of the equipment or system or through improvement in the work methodology with emphasis on pre-production arrangements. These modifications and improvements are preferably achieved through voluntary group activities. Work control in the field of production includes encouraging workers to exert efforts and make suggestions for improvement.

In order to further improve yield, it is advisable to install an inspection system to identify and remove defects at every work station. This is a feedback type quality control if looking downstream, but can be called a feed forward control when looking upstream. If economically feasible, it is recommended to automate such a control system.

Reductions in payments to suppliers should be achieved as a result of technical and managerial guidance on the part of the purchaser, and not by means of mere requests for cost reduction. The fruit of cost reduction efforts should be shared by the purchaser and the supplier. In some cases, financially stable suppliers with aggressive operational policies may initiate cost reduction efforts on their own and successfully introduce automatic equipment and related expertise from the equipment manufacturer.

6.2.2 Reduction in Labour and Indirect Costs

Reductions in labour cost should be considered in relation to depreciation cost. The introduction of automated equipment may reduce labour cost but would certainly inflate depreciation cost. If the inflation in depreciation cost exceeds the saving in wage payments, automation is not the way to cost reduction. On the other hand, wage payments can be reduced without appreciably inflating depreciation cost. Work efficiency can be enhanced either through improvement in work procedures or through additional attachments to the existing equipment. In these cases labour costs of affected sections can be reduced without sizable investments.

Wage cost reduction efforts discussed in this section, however, do not bring about reductions in wage payments per se, unless surplus labour is laid off. Wage cost reduction in one department usually means the surplus labour is absorbed by other departments. Curtailment of the labour force in one section without layoffs does not lead to the reduction in total labour cost unless the business is expanding.

Low depreciation of equipment is not a welcome phenomenon by itself except in a few special cases. Smaller weaving establishments attempt to use old machines rather than introduce depreciation-generating new machines. They do this through careful maintenance and adjustments in production work hours.

Finally, the smaller the indirect expense, the better. A certain plywood manufacturer of quality products decided to further reduce production cost through the utilization of advanced production techniques. He tried to decrease material and labour costs and boost the requipment operation rate. Then, the management drastically reduced the indirect cost by cutting a number of unnecessary managers in the field and in the offices. This immediately brought about a substantial profit.

Saving is also possible through reductions in sales expenses, general administrative expenses, and interest payments. Corporations can maintain a competitive edge through the elimination of unnecessary expenditures. In the production field, there appears to be plenty of "waste", "deviation from standards", and "strain".

When production management centres on cost, target figures are posted for carefully selected parameters, taking into account the influence on concerned parties. Once the targets have been reached, there is no turning back. Old target figures work as a basis for new target figures to realize further cost reduction and to beat competitors in an on-going cycle. The motivation and capability of people in the field is the basis for this type of management.

6.3 SMALL SCALE PRODUCTION OF A LARGE VARIETY OF PRODUCTS

6.3.1 Industrial Dynamics

An increase in the number of product types tends to inflate inventory.

This makes production more vulnerable to demand fluctuation. Industrial dynamics is an effective means of minimizing such vulnerability and is already exerting a far-reaching influence on industry.

Using simulation models, Professor J.W. Forrester of the Massachusetts Institute of Technology demonstrated that small changes in demand at the retail level can have a devastating effect on production when information is channeled to the production field through wholesale establishments and product warehouses.

The simulation models, taking into account the time required for information gathering and materials processing, demonstrated that a 10% increase in sales at the retail level increases factory production by 50%. If wholesalers are excluded from the information channel, fluctuation in production quantity is reduced by half. A number of corporations are actually making use of this theory demonstrated in the form of algebraic models. A certain manufacturer of decorative plywood operates a data collection system whereby orders from sales depots throughout the country are telexed into the production management department at the headquarters. These orders are compiled on a weekly basis for formulating production plans. This production management system is highly sensitive to demand fluctuation.

The automotive industry has a similar system in operation for some types of cars. Orders from dealers are telexed into the production management department of the car manufacturer. These data are analyzed and incorporated into the monthly production schedule in the form of specific scheduling to reflect demand in the market. Excessive production or a long delivery period due to inaccurate demand estimation is avoided in this way.

Professor Forrester has suggested that intermediation in the flow of information and goods may cause unnecessary distortion. He offered a solution to this abuse.

6.3.2 Inventory Reduction

This methodology works in the following manner. Suppose, one makes wooden tables. The table consists of four legs and a top. Tables are order made. If one does not purchase wood material or start production until a few days prior to the promised date of delivery to the customer, a big saving in inventory cost can be achieved. However, this type of production may not be economically efficient. The most economical production lot is the one in which the costs of inventory and set-up are minimized, and the production field traditionally adheres to this production lot. This production philosophy, however, assumes that there is a steady demand, which often is not the case. Therefore, when demand is fluctuating, this philosophy cannot work, and production upon receipt of order is usually more economical.

Corporations belonging to the Toyota family attempted to make small lot production economically viable by reducing the lot size. A smaller production lot means a smaller line inventory but more frequent line changes which are costly. The die change in stamping takes a considerable amount of time. If this time required for the die-change is fixed, the economic lot size can be easily derived, as it is a function of die change time and inventory costs. The smaller the values of these two parameters, the more economical is production. Figures 6-1 & 6-2 depict this relationship.

Figure 6-1 shows the average inventory of $\frac{Q}{2}$ for the production lot of Q is reduced to $\frac{Q}{4}$ when the production lot is halved to $\frac{Q}{2}$. This means the inventory is reduced in proportion to the size of the production lot. As indicated in Figure 6-2 inventory reduction itself can be achieved by curtailing set-up cost which decreases the size of the economical production lot. Through this methodology, Toyota made it possible to produce only ordered quantities. Even with assurance that the production in each lot is most economical, instability and diversification in customer needs can push the production lot size below the level of economic viability, assuming

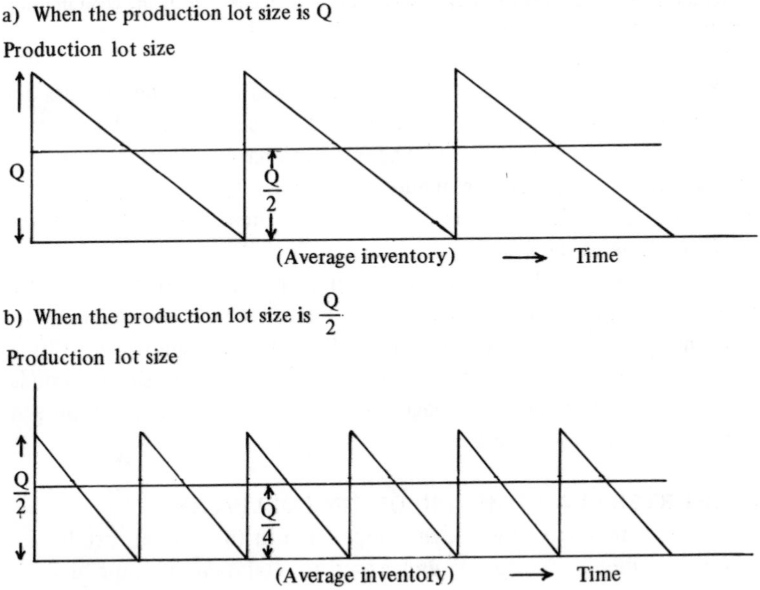

a) When the production lot size is Q

Production lot size

Q

$\frac{Q}{2}$

(Average inventory) ⟶ Time

b) When the production lot size is $\frac{Q}{2}$

Production lot size

$\frac{Q}{2}$

$\frac{Q}{4}$

(Average inventory) ⟶ Time

Figure 6-1 Relations between Production Lot and Inventory Volume

that production technologies remain the same. The shopfloor may be tempted to go into production of a lot based on expectations, resulting in increased inventory. Ideally, production should be completely adjustable to lot size fluctuation (See Figure 6-2).

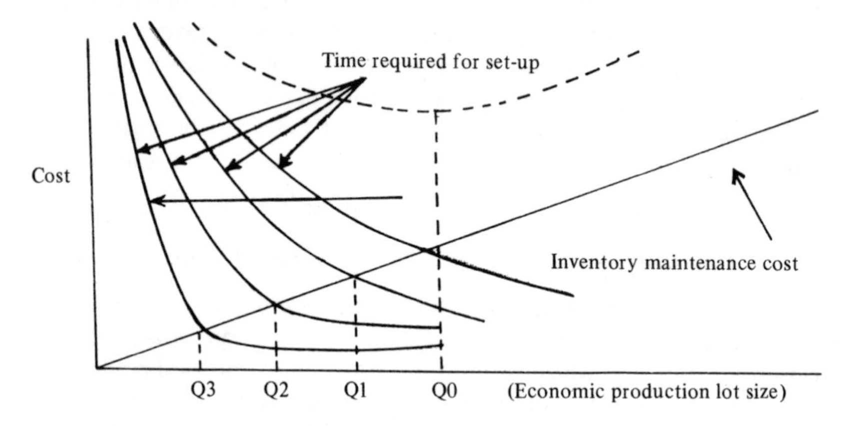

Figure 6-2 Economically Viable Production Lot v.s. Set-up Cost Curves

. . . . . . indicates the sum total of inventory maintenance cost and set-up cost. The lowest point of this curve corresponds to the most economical production lot. Improvements in set-up works to shift the cost curve to the left realizing economically viable production for smaller lots.

Reductions in set-up cost mean quicker and easier line changes for all types or sizes of equipment. Quicker line changes are the fruit of production system improvement. The revolutionary reduction in mould changing time for die casting made it possible to produce products in small losts at a profit. In terms of Figure 6-2, there has been a dramatic shift of the curve to the left.

The production lot needs to be further reduced if the customer requires more diversified product assortment. Smaller production lot size means not only reduced inventory volume but also shorter lead time. Diversified small quantity orders can be completed in short periods. Market-sensitive production management should realize a shift of production systems in this direction.

6.4 SHORTER LEAD-TIME AND ON-TIME DELIVERY

In order to survive the tough competition in the market, production management should constantly endeavour to maintain on time delivery using time-saving measures in each production phase. PERT is a technique used for such purposes.

PERT (Programme Evaluation and Review Technique) is said to have been introduced by the U.S. Navy in 1958. This technique focuses on delay-prone processes throughout the production flow. PERT sorts production processes into events and activities to form a network. An "event" means a work step and an "activity" corresponds to the time and resources required for shifting from one work step to another. Events and activities have "o" and "→" notations in the network.

The time required for each activity is estimated by application of the equation

$$t_e = \frac{t_o + 4t_m + t_p}{6}$$

where t_e is the mean elapsed time, t_o is the optimistic time estimate, t_m is the most likely time estimate, and t_p is the pessimistic time estimate. Experts' opinions are integrated to obtain workable t_o, t_m, and t_p values. The most time consuming process, called a "bottleneck," is identified in terms of the t_e value obtained. Then, activity variance is calculated for the bottleneck using the equation

$$\sigma^2 = \left(\frac{t_p - t_o}{6}\right)^2$$

where σ^2 is the estimated activity variance, and t_p and t_o are identical to t_p and t_o in the previous equation. Processes should be expedited for activities with large σ^2 values. Figure 6-3 indicates the critical path in this case is Ⓐ → Ⓓ → Ⓕ → Ⓖ, and improvement effort should be made on the Ⓓ → Ⓕ portion where the σ^2 value is higher compared with other activities.

A computer is used for lengthy computations covering complex networks. Networks consisting of thousands of events can be broken down into packages which are subject to independent analysis.

Although primarily concerned with lead time, PERT sometimes deals with the cost factor when certain activities have to be accelerated by mobilizing extra labour forces in cases of emergency. The analysis based on time and cost parameters is called PERT/COST. Consider a simple example of such analysis.

Let us assume the time and cost for both standard and emergency cases are known for the network in Figure 6-4. The bottleneck in this case is ① → ② → ④ → ⑤ which requires 16 weeks and ¥350,000. For 13-week delivery, the lead time should be shortened by three weeks. The most cost effective time reduction is attainable for the activities ④ → ⑤. No other cuts are needed to reduce the duration by three weeks. Cost information is the key for such analysis.

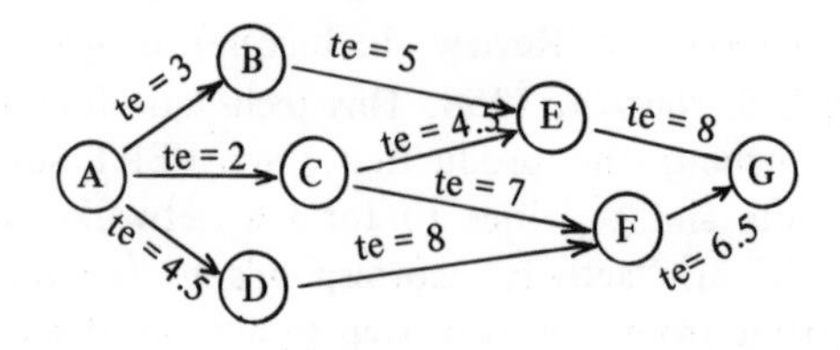

			t_o	t_m (weeks)	t_p	t_e	σ^2
(A)	→ (B)	Special component research	2	2	8	3	1.0
(B)	→ (E)	Supplier evaluation	3	4	11	5	1.8
(E)	→ (G)	Deliveries from suppliers	6	8	10	8	0.4
(A)	→ (C)	Basic design	2	2	2	2	0.0
(C)	→ (E)	Sub-contract specifications	3	4	8	4.5	0.7
(C)	→ (F)	Final design	5	7	9	7	0.4
(A)	→ (D)	Systems design	3	4	8	4.5	0.7
(D)	→ (F)	Systems tests	6	7	14	8	1.8
(F)	→ (G)	Production	5	6	10	6.5	0.7

Figure 6-3 PERT Network

Note: Quoted with modification from *Production Planning,* by Eiji Ogawa 1967, Kawade Shobo, p. 121

PERT and PERT/COST techniques are effective tools for production management of pre-production arrangements when delivery needs improvement due to demand fluctuation. For this reason, PERT will become more significant in the future.

6.5 HIGH QUALITY AND LOW PRODUCTION COST

Manufacturing corporations must respond to the demand for high quality products. However, with technical conditions remaining unchanged, quality improvement results in additional production cost. Assuming prices remain stable, better product quality should be achieved through improvement in technology. Quality circle activity at the shopfloor level

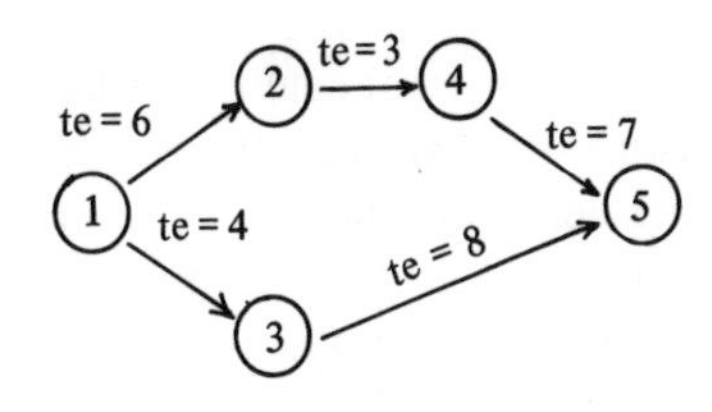

Activity	t_e		Cost		Cost Increase
	Standard	Express	Standard	Express	per week
	(weeks)		(¥00,000)		(¥00,000)
① → ②	6	4	10	14	2
① → ③	4	3	5	8	3
② → ④	3	2	4	5	1
③ → ⑤	8	6	9	12	1.5
④ → ⑤	7	4	7	8	0.33

Figure 6-4 PERT/COST Network

Source: Ogawa & Iwata, *An Introduction to Production Management,* Dobunkan, 1982 pp. 192-193.

is one means of improvement. The replacement of old type general-purpose machines with machining centres is another.

With improvements in product planning and design, higher quality and lower production cost can be further pursued upstream in the research and development stage. The key to effective quality management is the pursuit of this objective wherever and whenver possible throughout the entire production flow.

Furthermore, efforts should be made to maintain a fixed quality standard for a given period. Statistical quality control is used for this purpose. Statistical quality control, originated by Dr. W. Shewhart in 1931, was put to practical use in the United States during World War II and flourished in Japan in the postwar years. Today, Japan is considered to be the Mecca of quality control.

Statistical quality control consists primarily of random sampling and control charting. Random sampling is accomplished by selecting a few products at random for quality checks and evaluating the entire production lot on the basis of that quality check. Quality checking of every product is very expensive, and destructive types of quality checking are by nature not compatible with total checking. Random sampling is an economical compromise, beneficial to both the delivering and receiving sides. It is a trade off between the so-called produces' risk and the consumers' risk.

Producers' risk means the probability of a production lot being rejected despite having a satisfactory quality level. Likewise, consumers' risk is the probability of accepting products despite their unsatisfactory quality level. Prior to random checking, each producer and consumer have to agree on the definition of acceptable product quality in terms of the rejection rate per production lot and the number of samples to be checked per lot. For instance, a good product lot may be defined as a lot having a rejection rate of 2% or less and a bad product lot as having a rejection rate of 10% or more. In this case, if a standard one time random sampling is applied on the basis of the producer's risk of 5% and the consumer's risk of 10%, a production lot with four or more rejects out of sixty samples is a rejected lot. A JIS (Japanese Industrial Standard) table is applicable for this computation.

The control chart is also a tool used for statistical quality control. This method calls for deviation management within a designated control envelope based on the normal distribution curve. The mean value and the standard deviation are obtained on a normal distribution curve, and the events are controlled so that 95% happen within a range of $\pm 2\sigma$ of the target value. The quality is regarded to be acceptable if the actual measured value falls within this envelope. No further analysis is required. If measured values fall outside of the 2σ limit, actions should be taken to improve the situation without delay. Here the law of exceptions in business management theory is applied to quality control based on a statistical theory. (See Figure 6-5).

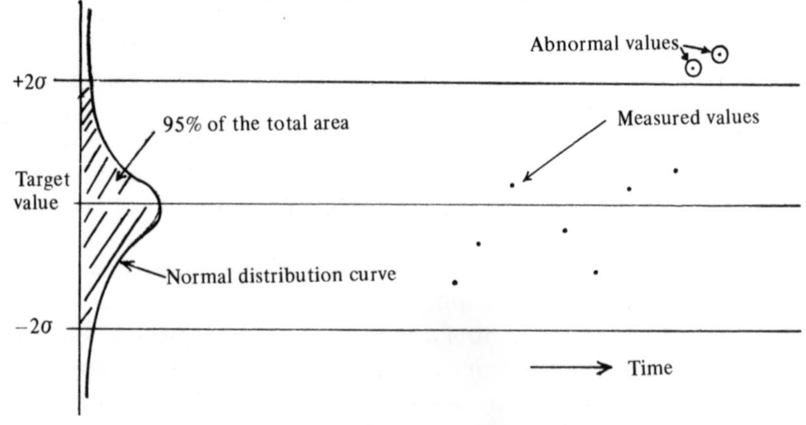

Figure 6-5 A Typical Control Chart

Quality assurance measures improve product quality as time passes and without raising production cost. The work force at the shopfloor level should be trained and motivated to bring about such a trend. In other words, success in production control depends on the people who are actually engaged in production. Quality circle activity plays an important role in this respect.

Product safety and reliability, prevalent demands in the market, should also be realized economically. That is why quality control is of vital importance in every stage of production.

6.6 SMALLER FIRMS IN UNSTABLE MARKETS

The market is equally demanding of small and medium-sized firms when it comes to production management, particularly for cost reduction. All cost items should be subject to strict control measures. Here small and medium-sized firms are characterized by low indirect costs compared with larger corporations. For smaller corporations, the first parameter to attempt is production yield which can be achieved by strengthening the field work force. Introduction of electronic devices is another means of curtailing labour cost and it should be considered as a way of structurally reinforcing small and medium sized enterprises.

Smaller firms should also endeavour to reduce inventories in order to realize small-scale production of a large variety of products economically. Points related to such endeavours were discussed in Section 3 of this chapter and will be discussed in Section 4 of Chapter 10. Time and quality control should be designed to realize shorter delivery periods, lower production costs, and improved product quality. Due to limited human resources, small corporations should exercise production management on a selective basis. In other words, quality control should be given priority for precision parts manufacturing, whereas scheduling control should be the most important parameter for time-critical production.

Particular emphasis should be placed on the determination to seek improvement. Stagnation means retardation in this competitive world.

Chapter 7
WORK STANDARDIZATION

Work standardization is the basis for production management. Work standards must be supported by all the parties concerned and should accommodate environmental changes. This chapter discusses traditional and synthesizing methods used for formulating work and time standards, and effects of learning experience, an increasingly important subject.

7.1 STANDARD: MEANING AND CONDITIONS

The word "standard" denotes a value measured according to a methodology agreed upon by concerned parties. "Standard value" includes the daily workload for a work team or an automated production system. The effort to realize this standard value is called standardization.

Although this chapter primarily deals with work standardization, standardization covers other production management parameters such as quality, time, quantity, cost, and profit. Standards are also set for factory environment and safety and sanitation at the work field. Since production management is an activity to improve the input-output relationship of physical and human energies used in every stage of production, it always pre-supposes a standard for improvement, a target value. In implementing production management, standards must be set in the first place.

Standards cannot always be quantified, as they often refer to methodologies and ways of thinking. (1) Quantifiable standards are called physical standards, (2) methodology-oriented standards are called behavioural standards, and (3) standards directing ways of thinking are called philosophical standards. Examples of these standards can be applied to work. A philosophical standard might be taking human dignity into consideration for work selection. An efficient, wasteless work methodology based on this philosophical standard, becomes the behavioural standard. The work procedure defines the number of product units and the time required to produce one product unit for the physical standard.

It is extremely important to break down standards into the three categories of philosophical, behavioural and physical, because standard time in the field becomes significant only if there exists proper philosophical and behavioural standards. Physical standards often go wild and torture workers unnecessarily. When behavioural standards are uncontrolled, people do not understand why they must follow a certain method in finishing their work. Physical and behavioural standards should be based on philosophical standards which are acceptable to all concerned parties. The standard time should provide work suitable for human beings. This is the first pre-requisite for effective standardization.

Second, a standard is meaningless unless it is accepted by the parties concerned. In one plant the author surveyed, he was astonished to find three different sets of standard time in use. The first set was proposed by production engineers, the second by cost analysts, and the third by workers at the shopfloor level. This was inevitable because the standards proposed by production engineers and cost analysts were unacceptable to the field workers.

Third, it is important to understand that a standard is not a rigid concept. In this era of rapid technological change, few things appear to remain static in the world of business. There has been a dynamic evolution in the ways of thinking in Japan. Even philosophical standards are changing, as well as behavioural and physical standards. It can be further argued that standards are here for the very purpose of better future transformation. After all, production management itself is a technique for improving the input-output relationship. Standards when defined as goals, need augmentation.

Fourth, as discussed thus far, the transformation of standards is unavoidable but needs to be initiated and implemented by those who are directly affected by standards. In the case of semi-automated man-machine systems, the field work force must take the initiative in formulating the work standards. Otherwise, it becomes difficult to ensure acceptance on the part of field workers.

At an automotive manufacturer, when proposing a change in work procedure, field supervisors must be able to demonstrate by themselves that the suggested change is feasible. This is necessary in order to convince workers and win their approval of the change.

7.2 FORMULATION OF WORK STANDARS – TRADITIONAL METHOD

7.2.1 Methodology Standardization

There are two types of work standardization – methodology standardization and time standardization. The first of these is based on the concept of healthy work. This idea was developed by Mr. and Mrs. F.B. Gilbreth who proposed 17 basic moves called Therblig, an anagram of their name. Their objective was to decompose all human behaviour into seventeen basic moves and establish optimal work methodologies by eliminating unnecessary moves. They first relied on visual observation of the work in progress, but latter ventured to take motion pictures. They devised means of facilitating the analysis of body movement and time relations by inserting time notations on the screen and changing the film speed when shooting. Such films are meticulously analyzed to determine standard methodologies.

7.2.2 Time Standardization

Optimal standard times are determined through 1) job timing, 2) ranking of the measurements, and 3) determination of the time tolerance.

A stopwatch is used for timing of each job. An average figure is obtained after repeated measurements. Time measurement figures thus obtained are then evaluated to see if they are acceptable as the standard times for each work element. Those figures deemed inappropriate are then levelled. This process is called ranking. Levelled figures are called normal times. This process is likely to provoke confrontation between labour and management since the union might not accept modified figures. A confrontation of this type should be solved by time synthesizing analysis which is discussed in the next section. Table 7-1 is a typical calculation. The co-efficient is less than 1 for below standard workers and more than 1 for above standard workers.

Table 7-1 Levelling of Measured Values

Work Element	Average Time (minutes)	Levelling co-efficient	Normal Time (minutes)
A	0.050	1.00	0.050
B	0.220	0.90	0.198
C	0.120	1.10	0.132
D	0.060	1.00	0.060
Average cycle time = 0.450		Aggregated normal time = 0.440	

The total of normal time figures for work elements is called the aggregated normal time which means the total work hours when standard workers work without interruption. However, there are inevitable delay factors in real life, such as: trips to the lavatory, repairs, machinery maintenance, let-ups in materials flows, delayed instructions, and adjustments of the equipment. Other interruptions are not considered inevitable, and therefore are not included in the standard time.

The standard time requirement is obtained as a sum total of time figures for set-up, processing and inevitable delays. It is difficult to determine the extent to which inevitable delays should be taken into consideration. In extreme cases, decisions are made as the result of political compromise between labour and management. Such compromises, however, may weaken the competitive edge of a corporation in the market. Therefore, it is recommended that labour and management reach agreements through a sampling method based on statistical theory.

According to this sampling method, the number of samples required for a desired level of reliability is determined through the application of bi-nomial distribution theory. For instance, the number of samples required for 95% reliability is obtained by the equation

$$a = \pm 2\sqrt{\frac{p(1-p)}{n}}$$

where, a is the absolute error against p (for instance the relative error of 5% correspond to an absolute error = 0.05 p), p is the probability of the event taking place, $(1 - p)$ is the probability of the event not taking place, and n is the number of samples. Solution of the above equation for n is expressed as:

$$n = \left(\frac{2}{a}\right)^2 p \cdot (1-p)$$

Assuming that $(1 - p)$, or inevitable delay, is 20%, p is 80% and a is 4%,

$$n = \left(\frac{2}{0.04}\right)^2 \times 0.8 \times 0.2 = 400$$

meaning that 400 samples are required.

Measurement is conducted on the basis of this calculation to determine "tolerance" with reference to normal time. The tolerance ratio is expressed as $\frac{1-p}{p}$ for known value of p. The standard time is calculated by the following equations.

$$\begin{aligned}\text{Standard time} &= \text{Normal time} + \text{inevitable delay}\\ &= \text{Normal time}\left(1 + \frac{\text{inevitable delay}}{\text{normal time}}\right)\\ &= \text{Normal time}\ (1 + \text{inevitable delay ratio})\end{aligned}$$

The standard time is subject to change due to work improvement and technological innovations. Japanese corporations have attempted to shorten the standard time by reducing the time required for set-up and processing and minimizing inevitable delays. Large equipment investment contributes much to the shortening of standard time and eventually to cost reduction. A corporation will lose international competitiveness if it adheres to the old standard time. One cannot expect smooth operation if standard time is determined unilaterally. There should be voluntary initiative for improvement from the shopfloor level. One should understand that production management is a brainchild of the search for pragmatism and the sentiment of working people.

7.3 TIME SYNTHESIZING ANALYSIS AND MULTI-UNIT SUPERVISION

7.3.1 Time Synthesizing Analysis

Traditional work standardization encountered the fierce resistance of labour unions regarding time measurement and the rating of average measurements. In order to overcome this difficulty, a new method was devised where a third party conducts work standardization independently from union and management. This new method is called time sythesizing analysis. A chart with time breakdown for all the motion elements is commercially available. Relative standard time values are synthesized into a total normal time value using this chart.

There are two representative methods of time synthesis. One is called MTM and the other WF. The former is used to explain the time synthesis methodology.

The MTM method was announced in the United States in 1948. Different time values are given depending on the distance and nature of the ten defined motions: (1) to reach, (2) to move, (3) to rotate, (4) to press, (5) to grasp, (6) to position, (7) to release, (8) to disengage, (9) to focus, and (10) to use legs and feet to move the body. For instance, the "reaching" motion can cover distances from 1 to 30 inches and is of five categories (A, B, C, D, and E). The time unit used in the MTM method is called TMU or time measurement unit which is $\frac{1}{10^5}$ hour or approximately $\frac{36}{1000}$ seconds. A chart of standard time values is obtainable from the MTM Association.

Let us apply MTM to pencil sharpening. The motion involved is very simple. One picks up an unsharpened pencil in the hand, sharpens it in the sharpener, and puts the pencil back in its original position. The breakdown of the motion and the related TMU values are shown on the purchased list. The TMU for the sharpening itself is defined separately according to the performance of the sharpener. Table 7-2 shows the process of arriving at the total normal time through the summation of individual TMUs. The two critical factors for MTM are the breakdown of motion and the allocation of TMU values corresponding to the performance of the equipment. This is particularly true in the pencil sharpening example shown in Table 7-2, where the TMU value of the sharpening motion is larger than the sum total of all other TMUs. Here, the performance capacity of the equipment is decisive.

Table 7-2 Time Standardization of Pencil Sharpening

Motion	TMU
1. *Reach* 4 inches for an un-sharpened pencil	8
2. *Grasp* one pencil (simple grasp)	2
3. *Move* the pencil 8 inches to the sharpener	12
4. *Position* the pencil in a manner for a loose fit	10
5. *Move* the pencil into the sharpener one inch	2
6. Sharpen the pencil	167
7. *Disengage* the pencil from sharpener (loose)	5
8. *Move* the sharpened pencil 8 inches to the original position	12
Total Normal Time	218 TMU

Note: Standard Time is the sum of total normal time and inevitable delay. This exercise was quoted from R. J. Hopeman, *Production Concepts-Analysis-Control,* C. E. Merrill Books, 1965.

7.3.2 Multi-Unit Supervision

In the case of automatic processing machines, the operator has nothing to do while the machine itself does the processing. Therefore, one operator can cover several machines and concentrate on set-up work. There is a division of labour between the operator and the machine. If it takes the operator 30 seconds to complete the set-up operation and move to the next machine, he can cover three machines, each with a process time of 60 seconds.

By decreasing the set-up time, the worker can cover four machines instead of three. The automation of work piece handling is actually attempted in manufacturing plants. If the set-up time, including the trip to the next machine, is reduced from 30 to 20 seconds, the same operator can cover four machines. A few seconds' improvement does not bring about appreciable results.

In order to increase the number of machines per operator, production should be automated further. First, machines should be connected to each other. Operators load work pieces at the beginning of the line of machines and unload finished pieces at the end. Such a processing line is called a transfer processing line. Dozens of machines are joined together to do a series of jobs with an operator doing the loading at the head of the line, and another doing the unloading at the end. A line capable of conducting different kinds of processing or processing of different types of product is called FMS (Flexible Manufacturing System).

The number of machines per operator can be increased through automation of set-up work. Surplus labour thus generated is used for supervision and maintenance, constant monitoring of the work process, and the provision of emergency measures. Eventually, physical contact between people and machines will be unnecessary except for maintenance. Workers' jobs in the future will consist of process improvement or replacement of processing machines or systems, review of pre-production arrangements, supervision, and maintenance.

P.H. Engelstad summarizes the basic points in designing workers' activities for higher motivation as follows:

(1) One worker can handle more than one job.
(2) The worker can and should learn on-the-job.
(3) Work contains meaningful decision making.
(4) Work can be considered meaningful to the well-being of the community.
(5) Work gives hope for the future.

Automation should progress in parallel with job restructuring. Work standards will undergo drastic changes both qualitatively and quantitatively. A lack of proper consideration of these points may provoke criticism of automation making the socio-technical approach (See Section 4-3 of Chapter 4) necessary.

7.4 LEARNING EFFECT

Jobs require learning by workers, particularly in job rotation. The management cannot afford to undertake unlimited training of workers in the face of severe market competition. It is quite natural that systematic control of the learning effect should be established. In other words, the standard time or work load should be set for workers in accordance with the progress of their learning.

The concept of a learning effect was first introduced by the aeronautical industry of the United States. As workers acquired experience in production, the time required to produce one plane was reduced. It is natural that they should discover the relationship between experience and productivity and utilize such a relationship in planning work load, scheduling, and personnel management.

An equation was devised to express this relationship (see Figure 7-1):

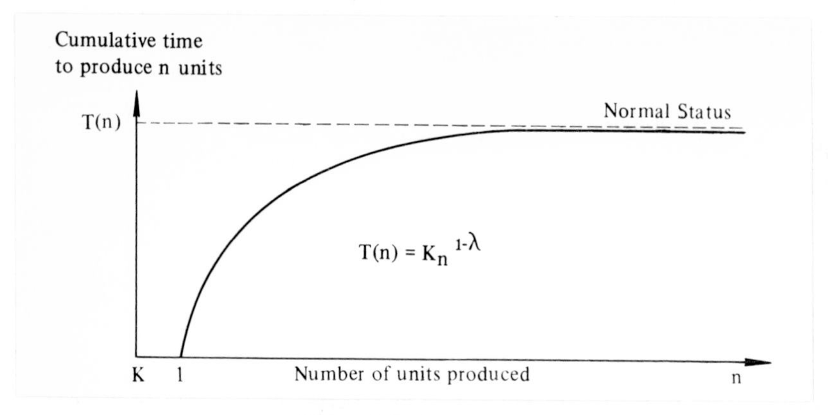

Figure 7-1 Learning Effect

Source: Martin K. Starr, *Operations Management,* Prentice-Hall, 1978, p. 479.

$$T(n) = K_n^{1-\lambda}$$

where, $T(n)$ is the cumulative time required to produce n units, K is the time required to produce the first unit, n is the number of units produced, and λ is the learning co-efficient defined as $0 \leqq \lambda \leqq 1$
if $\lambda = 0$,

$$T(n) = nK$$

which means that the time required to produce one unit remains unchanged. In other words, $T(n)$ does not converge if $\lambda = 0$. If λ is nearly equal to 1, the curve rapidly converges to the normal status line in Figure 7-1. The larger the value of λ, the more rapidly the learning is completed.

In order to use this cumulative production time $T(n)$ in the field, it is convenient to obtain average production time $\overline{T}(n)$, expressed in the following equation:

$$\overline{T}(n) = \frac{T(n)}{n} = K^{n-\lambda}$$

A logarithmic transformation makes the actual calculations a matter of single subtraction:

$$\log \overline{T}(n) = \log K - \lambda \log n$$

Let us take a simple example based on the figures in Table 7-3. These figures are approximated by the function $\overline{T}(n) = K_n^{\lambda}$. Using the least squares method, λ is obtained as 0.8. K is known to be 500 hours. Therefore,

$$\overline{T}(n) = 500 \times n^{-0.8}$$

or, $$\log \overline{T}(n) = \log 500 - 0.8 \log n$$

Table 7-3 Production Data

Month	Number of cumulative production units (n)	Average Production Time $(\bar{T}(n))$
		hrs.
April	10	79.25
May	50	21.87
June	100	12.56
July	200	7.22
August	400	4.14
September	1,000	1.99

The production time is 500 hrs. when $n = 1$.

If the parent company pays for the production time of ten hours, the subcontractor should cumulatively produce 133 units to meet the time expectation. In other words, the minimum order should be for 133 units. The same solution is obtainable by using a full logarithmic graph.

Because of the prevailing trend towards multi-variety-small-lot production, it is becoming increasingly important to analyse such a learning effect in work standardization. However, this is not a panacea. For instance, learning co-efficient based on old data is of questionable merit when applying the technique to new jobs. Jobs are subject to constant improvement based on past experience. In extreme cases, the only viable data may be obtainable from the most recent experience.

With its emphasis on the concept of man-hours, the learning effect of direct workers may not be greatly improved in the case of highly automated production systems. A considerable number of man-hours may be necessary on the part of engineers, technicians, and field supervisors to realize even a moderate improvement. Therefore, too much attention to the learning effect experienced by direct workers gives only one side of the picture.

Incorporation of the learning effect in job analysis encourages workers' initiative towards work improvement. With autonomous work management, which is gaining momentum, it is important for workers to accelerate their learning ability as a means of achieving management objectives.

7.5 WORK STANDARDIZATION IN SMALL AND MEDIUM-SIZED FIRMS

Standardization is the starting point for work management. Without a standard, there would be no management of the work field. Small and medium sized firms in Japan owe their growth to the rigorous enforcement of advanced quality control techniques. This is a major reason why larger corporations in Japan have decided to utilize suppliers rather than depending on inhouse production. Quality means satisfying customers needs for accuracy and durability. Furthermore, high yield is a prerequisite for making the supplier business profitable.

When the production line is partially automated, the establishment of an optimal work standard and the faithful observation of it is the key to high yields. It should be stressed once again that work standards are subject to constant improvement. Proper training on production techniques, and work management should be given to nurture a capable field work force. If this procedure is implemented successfully by the management, workers will take the initiative in work standard improvement through group emulation.

It is also recommended that small and medium sized firms use time synthesizing analysis for job standardization. Their production lots are getting increasingly smaller and non-repetitive. It is desirable, therefore, to make full use of learning effects in the deployment of production management.

Chapter 8
PRODUCTION PLANNING

In this chapter, the four subjects to be discussed are: long, medium and short-term production planning; simplified short-term planning based on man-hours and linear programming; simulation models for production planning at the factory level; and sales forecasting as a basis for production planning.

8.1 WHAT IS PRODUCTION PLANNING?

8.1.1 Categorization

Production planning refers to integrated efforts at high levels in the corporation and not to implementation of programmes at the shopfloor level. Production planning is typically carried out at the corporate, divisional (profit centre), and factory levels for long (5 years), medium (2 years), and short (less than a year) terms.

There are numerous parameters related to long-term production plans. Typically, such parameters include factory location, product type, production capacity, plant layout, equipment type, building design, and number of production personnel. The factory location may be overseas. The inauguration of commercial production of new products as a result of R & D efforts should naturally be included in such production plans. In this case, focal points are not only the planning of production itself, but also the planning for each stage of production, pre-production arrangements, product planning, design, and research and development.

Medium-term production plans do not deal with new product development or plant construction. Typical parameters would cover model change, modification in production capacity, factory layout change, building expansion, building renovation, and personnel relocation. These production plans focus on the modification of long-term plans on a two-year basis.

Short-term production plans are implementation oriented. There are execution programmes for six-month, three-month, and one-month periods under the framework of one-year production plans. One-year programmes may include minor model changes, partial modification of production capacity, and limited renovation of the equipment layout or factory building. It is not easy to draw a clear demarcation line between short-term and medium-term plans. One of the reasons is that factory building and equipment may be renovated in a short period of time through the employment of advanced technologies.

Three-month and six-month execution programmes are more specifics oriented and, therefore, cover a much smaller number of parameters. The production system stays intact with the exception of very minor changes. The major parameters will include the number of employees, production speed, overtime work, work volume of suppliers, and inventory.

The size of the work force is adjustable by hiring or discharging part-time workers and through the relocation of full-time workers. Production speed is also adjustable to a certain extent depending on the volume of order bookings. A certain amount of overtime work may be utilized. However, three hours overtime every work day for a month would adversely affect the workers health and be disadvantageous to the corporation from the standpoint of cost effectiveness.

One month is the shortest feasible term for integrated execution of a programme. Certain corporations call this a "confirmed" programme. In this case, variables are restricted to production speed, overtime work hours and orders to suppliers. Machine allocation is finalized according to this confirmed programme. At this stage, local contingency measures are of vital importance.

8.1.2 How to Interprete Production Plans

Short-term production plans are easy to understand as there are only a limited number of variables. Assuming a constant number of overtime work hours and volume of orders to suppliers, short-term production plans are defined as a function with four variables: number of workers (W_t), production volume (P_t), inventory (I_t), and sales volume (S_t), "t" being a specified business term or time period covered by the production plan. As mentioned earlier, type of production can either be job-order production or production to stock. Assuming that this production is job-order type,

$$P_t = S_t$$

In other words, the production for the "t"th business term is equal to the sales volume for the same term. If S_t fluctuates, so does P_t. P_t increases or decreases in direct proportion to S_t, (except in the case where the variance in S_t is absorbed by the volume of order to suppliers). If

P_t fluctuates as a result of change in S_t, W_t also varies accordingly.

If W_t is fixed, P_t is the maximum production. (Here again, the case of extra overtime work to increase production is disregarded).

Production to stock assumes a constant annual demand,

$$P_t = P_{t-1},$$

which means the production volume is the same as in the previous term. If S_t decreases, I_t increases. If S_t increases far beyond expectation, I_t becomes zero. However, W_t does not fluctuate, which means the employment is stable.

Although excessive inventory (I_t) is regarded as undesirable, seasonal variation is an effective means of adjusting constant production to cyclic demand fluctuation. In this case, there is a planned inventory fluctuation according to demand estimation. Since S_t in the above equation is basically an estimation of sales, the given value is rarely accurate in real life. Therefore, W_t and/or I_t fluctuate in either type of production when S_t fluctuates.

The production manager should attempt to realize minimum cost fluctuation relative to changes in W_t and I_t. The actual practice in manufacturing business is a hybrid of job-order production and production to stock which appears to be the answer to unexpected fluctuation in S_t. In other words, there exists a production format with an optimal hybrid ratio. The activities relative to these parameters can be called the planning of the production format (see Figure 8-1).

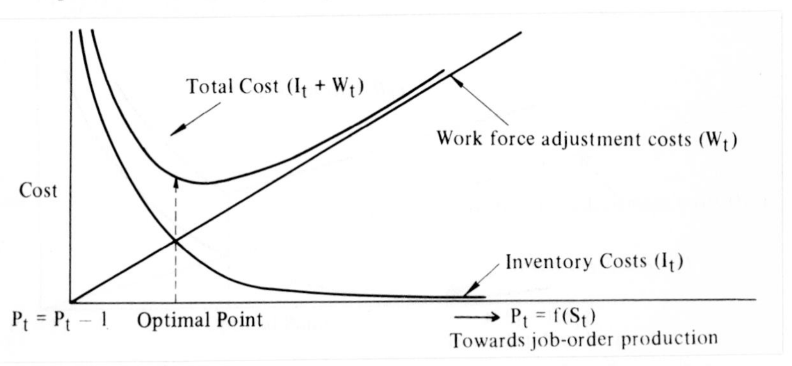

Figure 8-1 Optimum Production Format Planning

Source: Martin K. Starr, *Operations Management,* Prentice-Hall, 1978, p. 265.

The number of overtime hours and the volume of orders to suppliers should be taken into consideration in production planning.

W_t and P_t can be expressed as

$$W_t = W_t' + \widetilde{W}_t$$
$$P_t = P_t' + \widetilde{P}_t$$

where, W_t' denotes the number of workers not working overtime, $\widetilde{W}_t$ is the number of workers working overtime, P_t' is the volume of inhouse production, and $\widetilde{P}_t$ is the volume of orders to suppliers.
In job-order production,

$$P_t' + \widetilde{P}_t = S_t$$

which means inhouse production and orders to suppliers are variables to accommodate fluctuation in S_t. Inhouse production can be adjusted by regulating the overtime work force ($\widetilde{W}_t$) or the number of regular workers (W_t'). In production to stock,

$$P_t' + \widetilde{P}_t = P_{t-1'} + \widetilde{P}_{t-1}$$

Although I_t increases in theory when S_t decreases, the increase in I_t would not directly reflect the decrease in S_t because the management would certainly attempt to reduce overtime work and orders to suppliers to mitigate the impact on inventory. The reverse situation takes place when S_t increases. In other words, there are a variety of buffers between sales and production volumes. These buffers should be fully utilized from an overall standpoint. However, if one's orders to suppliers are reduced to zero during a recession, the suppliers will not accept orders when the economy recovers. There must exist close interdependence between parent companies and their suppliers despite the fact suppliers are a means of adjusting production to sales. This makes production management even more difficult and complicated.

8.2 PRODUCTION PLANNING METHODOLOGIES

8.2.1 Planning by Manhours

Although complex methodologies using computers are effective means of production planning, plant managers often resort to simplified production planning techniques based on manhours when programming production for a month or three months.

Here, the concept of a manhour is critical, because different products and processes are expressed in one parameter. A plant manager may say, "We need 120,000 manhours for next month's production, but can afford only 100,000 manhours inhouse. Therefore, we need 20,000 manhours from our suppliers." Assuming one month consists of 20 working days and each working day has eight working hours, 750 full-time workers are required to digest 120,000 manhours a month if the quality of labour is not taken into account:

120,000 manhours/8 hours × 20 days = 750 (workers)

If there are only 625 workers in this plant, the number of manhours consumable per month with this workforce is 100,000 (8 hours × 20 days × 625 workers), which is 20,000 short of the target. This gap should be bridged either through overtime or utilization of suppliers. The plant manager's remark is in reference to this situation. The next months schedule for overtime work or orders to suppliers are set accordingly.

Let us discuss inhouse manhour management under a different situation as prescribed in Table 8-1.

Table 8-1 Production Planning by Manhour

Production Programme for the Nth Month

Product Type	Quantity	Manhour per Product	Total Manhour
A	100	100	10,000
B	200	50	10,000
C	200	45	9,000
		Grand Total:	29,000

Assuming one month consists of 25 working days and each day has 8 working hours, the number of workers required to consume 29,000 manhours is 145. If there are only 130 workers, 90% of whom report to work each working day, this factory is short 28 workers per day or 5,600 manhours per month. According to Japanese labour law, overtime remuneration on workdays is 50% more than regular hourly wages, and on Sundays and national holidays, twice the regular payment amount. Therefore, extensive use of overtime work means a considerable rise in production cost. In this case, workers are expected to work 25 days a month, the maximum number of overtime affordable per worker being 20 hours, which means 2,340 manhours per month (117 workers × 20 hours). This still leaves 3,260 manhours (5,600 – 2,340) to be filled in some way. The plant manager may utilize the suppliers. Production on short notice often results in higher production cost so suppliers should be notified well in advance.

If there is sufficient lead time of, say three months, the hiring of part-timers, seasonal workers or the aged may be the solution, provided the production process is structured to absorb an inexperienced labour force.

State-of-the-art production management assumes manhour planning and rechecking every three months. Introduction of the linear programming technique assists plant managers in minimizing production cost in a volatile production environment. It represents a more detailed computation than this simple method using manhours.

8.2.2 Linear Programming

Linear programming is a technique devised to minimize production cost for a short period of time ranging from three to twelve months. Linear programmes, especially the transportion method, is easy to understand. Principles are simple although computation is rather complicated. One can always use a computer to facilitate the computation.

Let us examine the basic philosophy of linear programming as applied to a three-month production period. If monthly demand for the product is fixed, the most economical way is to meet the demand with normal production capacity. Since demand constantly fluctuates in real life, employees would have to work overtime or outside help such as part-timers and suppliers could be used. If plans are made well in advance, surplus labour may be utilized for a month to produce goods deliverable a month or two months later, depending on the cost required for such extra work. This relationship is explained by the linear programming technique, where

- I_o = inventory at the beginning of the term,
- R_i = normal production capacity for the "i"th term,
- O_i = additional production capacity due to overtime for the "i"th term,
- T_i = suppliers' production capacity for the "i"th month,
- n = the number of months in the "i"th term,
- S_i = demand for the "i"th term,
- I_i = inventory at the end of the term,
- C_R = production cost corresponding to normal production capacity,
- C_o = production cost corresponding to overtime production,
- C_T = payments to suppliers, and
- C_i = inventory cost per product unit per month.

Production and inventory can respond to the demand for the first month. From the second month on, the production, including output from suppliers and overtime work, plus any inventory accumulated during previous months are used to satisfy the monthly demand. The cost breakdown is shown in Table 8-2.

Monthly production volume is set as a function of capacity and demand. Production cost for the monthly production volume thus obtained should be minimized. Details of equations and calculations will not be explored, but roughly speaking, arbitrary production figures are to substitute notations other than M's in the table. Optimal production formats are determined on a monthly basis using the transport solution

Table 8-2 Production Cost Analysis

		1st term	2nd term	3rd term	Term end inventory	Slack	Capacity
Inventory at beginning of term		0	C_I	$2C_I$	$3C_I$	0	I_0
1st month,	normal work	C_R	$C_R + C_I$	$C_R + 2C_I$	$C_R + 3C_I$	0	R_1
	overtime	C_o	$C_o + C_I$	$C_o + 2C_I$	$C_o + 3C_I$	0	O_1
	suppliers	C_T	$C_T + C_I$	$C_T + 2C_I$	$C_T + 3C_I$	0	T_1
2nd month,	normal work	M	C_R	$C_R + C_I$	$C_R + 2C_I$	0	R_2
	overtime	M	C_o	$C_o + C_I$	$C_o + 2C_I$	0	O_2
	suppliers	M	C_T	$C_T + C_I$	$C_T + 2C_I$	0	T_2
3rd month,	normal work	M	M	C_R	$C_R + C_I$	0	R_3
	overtime	M	M	C_o	$C_o + C_I$	0	O_3
	suppliers	M	M	C_T	$C_T + C_I$	0	T_3
Demand		S_1	S_2	S_3	I_3	Slack	Total

M denotes prohibitive cost. For instance, the production during the 2nd term cannot satisfy demand for the first term.

method for the purpose of minimizing overall production cost. A computer is used for this computation. Provided all sales and cost assumptions are correct, utmost cost reduction is automatically guaranteed.

8.3 SIMULATION MODELING

Despite the assumption in Section 8.2 that production plans are drawn by the plant manager, some ingenious people thought it might be possible to let a computer do the planning. Professor E.H. Bowman of the United States devised a model depicting a plant manager's decision making process in production planning. Professor Bowman assumed the plant manager formulates production plans based on fluctuations in sales and inventory, provided the production system remains unchanged. The impact of fluctuation in sales is expressed in the equation

$$P_t = S_t + x(P_{t-1} - S_t)$$

All notations in this equation, with the exception of x, were defined in the provious section of this chapter. x in this equation is a co-efficient arbitrarily quantified by the plant manager in the range of 0 to 1. If x equals 1, the equation reads:

$$P_t = S_t + 1x(P_{t-1} - S_t) = P_{t-1}$$

which represents constant production to stock. If x equals 0 the equation reads:

$$P_t = S_t$$

which means job-order production. In other words, this co-efficient represents the plant manager's arbitrary choice of the type of production. If the plant manager decides to set the co-efficient at 0.5, 50% of the production will be job-order type while the rest will be production on stock.

$$P_t = S_t + 0.5\,x(P_{t-1} - S_t)$$
$$= \frac{S_t + P_{t-1}}{2}$$

In this case, the sum total of estimated sales and production of the previous term is divided by two, indicating that the plant managers decision is at the mid-point between job-order production and production to stock.

Inventory is expressed in the equation:

$$P_t = S_t + y(I_N - I_{t-1})$$

where I_N = standard inventory,

y = a co-efficient reflecting the degree of inventory control in the production plan. The value of y is arbitrarily set by plant manager between 0 and 1. If $y = 0$, $P_t = S_t$, which means inventory has nothing to do with production planning i.e., job order production. If $y = 1$,

$$P_t = S_t + 1 \times (I_N - I_{t-1})$$
$$= S_t + I_N - I_{t-1}$$

If $I_N < I_{t-1}$,

$$(I_N - I_{t-1}) < 0$$

which means that inventory has a negative impact on production, whereas

if $I_N > I_{t-1}$

$$(I_N - I_{t-1}) > 0$$

which means that inventory has a positive impact on production.

The two equations above express relations between production, estimated sales, and production and inventory which may be integrated to a composite equation,

$$P_t = S_t + x(P_{t-1} - S_t) + y(I_N - I_{t-1})$$

The plant manager chooses arbitary values for x and y in his decision-making. Professor Bowman's explanation for the estimation of S_t for terms subsequent to the "t"th term will not be elaborated, but, unexpectedly good results were obtained by substituting actual figures for the variables in the above composite equation. This technique opened the way for computerization of simulation models of production planning.

8.4 ESTIMATION OF SALES

The estimation of sales is the basis for production planning. Its accuracy is reflected directly in the viability of the production plan.

Normally, the two methods of sales estimation are top-down and bottom-up. In the top-down method, the growth rate of the industry is obtained based on some macroscopic figures such as estimated growth rate of GNP. Then, the sales volume of a corporation is estimated on the basis of its market share within the industry. In the bottom-up method, sales estimation is made by the corporate sales force, product by product, and integrated into an estimate. The two sets of estimated figures obtained through these contrastive methods will usually not agree with each other. It is the role of the management to bridge the gap between the two.

There are two types of implementation; formal and informal, the former meaning systematic implementation at the corporate level. The latter is often conducted by proprietors of smaller firms, invariably producing more accurate results compared with formal implementation.

Formal implementation includes quantitative and non-quantitative modeling. Quantitative modeling includes regression analysis, quantum economic modeling, data extrapolation, and index averaging, the last two being sequential analysis techniques. Non-quantitative modeling includes interviews with customers, testing through fictitious markets, and testing through actual markets. In this section, three popular techniques belonging to non-quantitative modeling are discussed and regression analysis, a technique belonging to quantitative modeling, is briefly reviewed.

8.4.1 Interviews

Sales persons or specialists conduct interviews to estimate explicit and implicit demand. This is the most common method used extensively in industry. Care should be taken on the following points to increase the accuracy of estimation:

Does the sample adequately represent population?

Hypothetical questions tend to draw hypothetical answers. This is particularly true of new products.

Interviewees tend to give answers pleasing to the interviewer.

Answering questions is one thing but making an actual purchase is another.

Are the questions understood by the interviewee?

8.4.2 Testing Through Simulated Marks

This method requires organization of a simulated market with a limited number of consumers engaged in the purchasing activity in order to evaluate the impact of new products, pricing, and advertising on target consumers. This is an effective method of demand estimation provided careful consideration is given to the following points:

Purchasing behaviour in an artificial environment is different from purchasing behaviour in real life.

The participants tend to satisfy the intention of the market organizer. For instance, if the experiment is on the price reduction of a certain product, participants tend to buy that particular product.

8.4.3 Testing Though Actual Markets

This technique, often used for testing new products, is also applicable for price change and other promotional policies on the part of the distributor. In this case, new activities take place in a specifically defined market to obtain a "feel". Sometimes, two identical markets are chosen for the sake of comparison with promotional activities taking place in only one of the two. More objective evaluation on new pricing, new products, and new advertising is obtained in this way, compared with the former method of selecting only on test market.

However, a number of problems need to be solved for truly viable evaluation.

8.4.4 Regression Analysis

Regression analysis is frequently used as a means of quantitative estimation. A linear equation is often assumed with a small number of variables.

$$S = A_0 + A_1X_1 + A_2X_2 + \ldots\ldots A_nX_n + e$$

where S = estimated sales

A_n = a co-efficient

X_n = a variable affecting S, and

e = error

Another equation often used for regression analysis is:

$$S = B_0Z_1^{B1}Z_2^{B2} + \ldots\ldots Z_n^{Bn}\mu$$

The logarithmic version of the above, called a polynominal regression, represents a linear relationship.

$$\log S = \log B_0 + B_1 \log Z_1 + B_2 \log Z_2 + \ldots\ldots B_n \log Z_n + \log \mu$$

which is identical to the above first linear equation except that this one is in a logarithmic format.

It appears that the simple regression formula of $S = A_0 + A_1X_1 + e$ is useful generally for analytical purposes. For given data, A_0 and A_1 are determined through the least squares method. The viability of the solution thus obtained is often expressed in terms of the co-efficient of determination which can vary within range of 0 to 1. The closer the co-efficient is to 1, the more viable is the solution.

8.5 PRODUCTION PLANNING FOR SMALLER FIRMS

Production plans could cover any period of time but should be formulated in an integrated fashion. When smaller firms are engaged in multi-variety-small lot production, production planning on the basis of manhours may be most effective. In order to survive in an extremely competitive environment, smaller firms must employ multi-variety-small-lot production. It is of vital importance for smaller firms to reduce the number of manhours through proper production planning.

As discussed in Section 8.1, the production of smaller firms in actual practice should be a hybrid of job-order production and production to stock. The selection of a proper mix between these two formats is another factor subject to critical business decisions. The basic guideline appears to be the realization of a job-order format with a short delivery period and low cost. Low cost production to stock assumes a large production lot and intensive utilization of the learning effect. Inventory cost should be taken into consideration in passing final assessment on this type of production in comparison with job-order production. The Toyota Production System achieved a happy marriage between the two concepts. Job-order production is applied to its maximum extent. This point will be further discussed in Section 4 of Chapter 9 and Section 4 of Chapter 10.

If smaller firms depend completely on job-order production, do they still need sales estimation? The answer is in the affirmative. When it comes to equipment, quick modification is not possible. Plans for the hiring of outside help such as part-timers and suppliers should be laid out well in advance to ensure smooth execution. Therefore, it is important for smaller firms to search the way for economical operation against the background of developments in their particular industry.

Chapter 9
SCHEDULING AND INVENTORY CONTROL

Scheduling and inventory control is implemented on the basis of a production plan. This chapter deals with Materials Requirements Planning (MRP) and its relation to multi-variety small lot production, scheduling control in relation to different production formats, and inventory control. Then, the application of the Gantt Chart and ABC analysis are discussed for possible implementation in smaller business entities.

9.1 INTRODUCTION

9.1.1 Scheduling Control

Long-term production plans are segmented into short-term plans for implementation purposes. Integrated as they are, production plans need to be broken down to specifics at the point of implementation. In other words, specific goals should be established for scheduling and inventory control.

The production plan provides basic goals for the scheduling control situated immediately below it. Scheduling control consists of materials requirements planning (hereafter called MRP), coordination with respect to production capacity, and detailed scheduling. The control process should cover the machinery workload, launching, and progress. Section 9.2 deals primarily with MRP and Section 9.3 discusses watchpoints related to the implementation of the detailed work schedule (see Figure 9-1).

Scheduling control aims at two things, the shortening of lead time and delivery period, and the realization of the promised delivery date. This process may include the shortening in production time based on improvements and renovations in pre-production arrangements. A short delivery period is possible only through improvements at the shopfloor level, namely the reduction in time required for set-up, processing and queue time.

9.1.2 Inventory Control

Inventory control listed on the right hand side of Figure 9-1 is indispensable to scheduling control. Production plans and detailed work

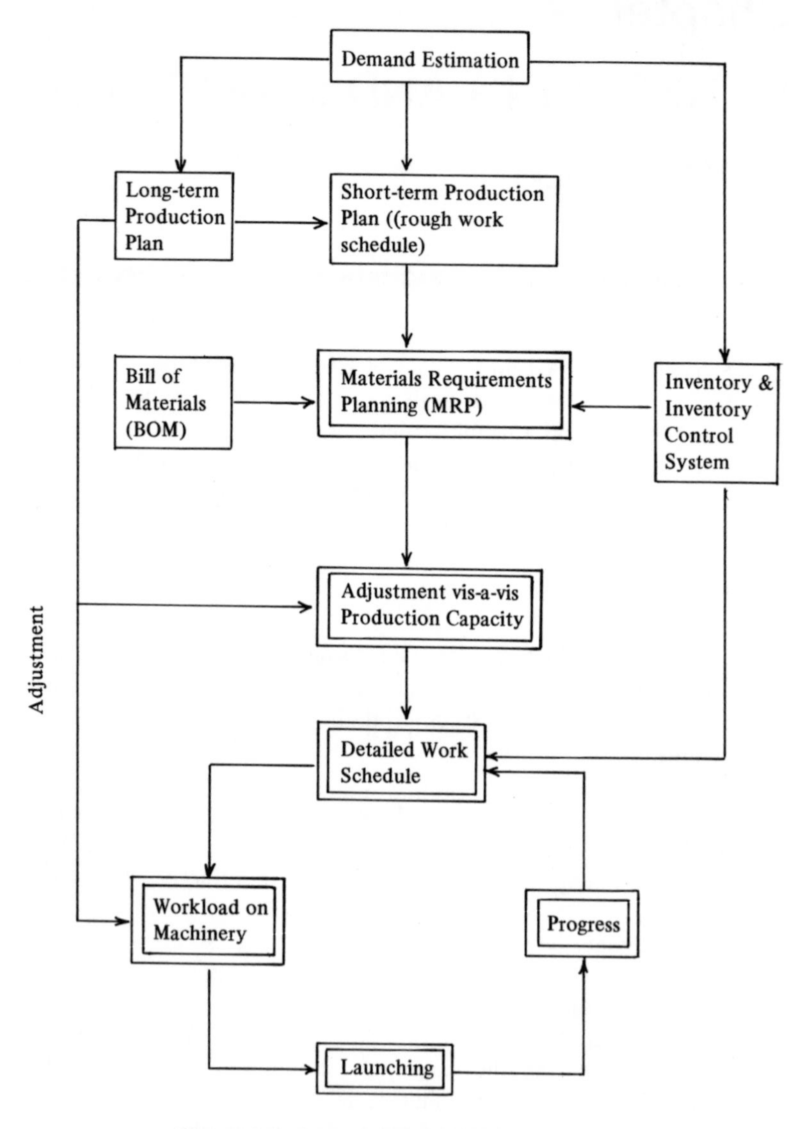

Figure 9-1 Concept of Schedulign Control

Items in double rectangular frames are subject to scheduling control.

schedules are formulated on the basis of inventory. In this case, inventory is controlled according to the inventory control plan. The smaller the standard inventory, the better, for a small inventory means low cost. Rent on the inventory yard, the interest payment on bank loans, and possible obsolescence of the inventory are among the costs and risks related to a large inventory.

There are many inventory considerations, including both quality and quantity. Inventory includes materials, purchased parts, work in process, half-finished products, tools, products, and other related materials. Systematically, these kinds of inventory are classified into purchased goods, line inventory, and products. Therefore, inventory control encompasses purchasing, production, and sales. Inventory is generated because purchasing and production take place in a lot. On the other hand, inventory is necessary because customers do not want to wait for the entire production period after ordering. Furthermore, inventory is necessary as a buffer against uncertain deliveries from suppliers, unexpected delay in production, and inaccurate estimation of demand.

The optimal level of inventory differs from one corporation to the next, but corporations generally tend to hold unnecessarily large inventories.

There are two objectives of inventory control, (1) inventory reduction, and (2) maintenance of standard inventory level. Inventory reduction is achieved primarily through improvements in purchasing, production, and sales activities. It is equally important to preclude unnecessary inventory and maintain standard inventory level through the rigorous implementation of an inventory control system.

While adhering to the standard inventory level, bear in mind that inventory control is related to goods and materials in substance. It is not easy to take an accurate count of stock, particularly when a large number of types and items are involved. A regular inventory check is an indispensable part of inventory control.

9.2 MATERIALS REQUIREMENTS PLANNING

Materials requirements planning, or MRP, has been placed in the limelight because manufacturing processes have become extremely complex. A complex manufacturing process encompasses a large number of parts which are assembled into subassemblies and then into finished products according to a strictly observed sequence. Proper selection of this sequence brings about appreciable reduction in inventory. Scheduling control, calling for production of the required quantity when needed, is in conformity with the concept of inventory reduction which is the very basis of inventory control.

Observing the production line structure shown in Figure 9-2 for product A, consisting of subassemblies B, C, and D, one can tell that subassembly D at level 3 should be launched five weeks prior to the final assembly at level zero based on the time requirements for each subassembly indicated in weeks in the figure. The calculations make it extremely difficult to implement MRP for a precision product consisting of a large number of subassemblies and components.

Figure 9-2 shows different levels of processing and assembly. Level zero is the final assembly and level one is the highest level of subassembly or processing. The number of relative parts increases as one goes down to levels 2 and 3. Note that common parts are needed in different levels; for instance, part B is needed at levels one and two, and part D at levels two and three, indicating the need for early production planning for those parts.

Figure 9-3 shows how many parts B, C, and D are needed, and when, in order to produce 100 units of A which is the final product. The production of parts B and C should begin in the fourth week because two weeks are necessary to complete those parts. The production of D should start in the third week for level two, in preparation for B at level one. At level two, the production of D and B should start in the third and the second weeks, respectively, in preparation for C at level one. Likewise, the production of D at level three should begin in the first week in preparation for B at level two.

To recap, the production should begin for 100 D's in the first week, for 200 B's in the second week, for 200 D's in the third week, and for 100 B's and 200 C's in the fourth week in order to start assembling 100 A's at the beginning of the sixth week. No subassembly is launched in the fifth week.

If two units of B and four units of C are required every week as spare parts, the MRP network in Figure 9-3 needs minor modifications. Production of such a small quantity had better be implemented collectively in one of the weeks. In planning MRP, the cases such as this require attention.

MRP appears to be suited for application in the automotive industry. Due to its proven effectiveness, the MRP methodology is finding new applications for the management of work force, equipment, administrative and technical capabilities, investment, and cash flow. These new application are called resources requirements planning (RRP).

9.3 SCHEDULING CONTROL

9.3.1 Small Lot Production

At the implementation stage of detailed scheduling, specific

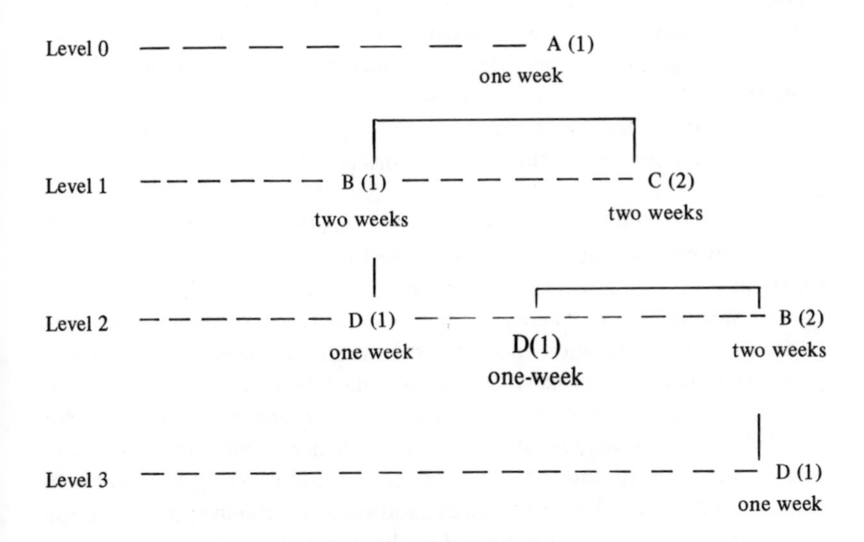

Figure 9-2 An Example of MRP

Note: The numbers in brackets denote the number of subassembly units or parts. The weeks show the time required to assemble one unit of finished product.

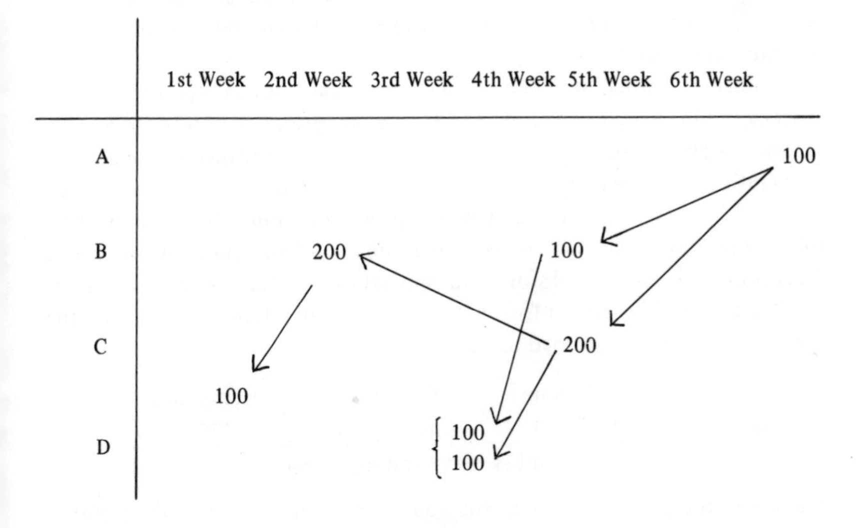

Figure 9-3 MRP Calculation

instructions should be given on what to produce, how much, when, and how. These instructions are obtainable through examination of MRP data relative to product type, delivery, quantity, and inhouse capacity mobilization or subcontractor services. Bills of materials and detailed job descriptions should accompany the final production instructions.

In small lot production, which normally is of job order type, the production plan is formulated on the basis of the delivery date in the purchase order. Line allocation should be made between orders, which is likely to generate line inventory in the form of semi-finished products. Customers do not give orders that optimize line allocation on the part of the manufacturer. Therefore, the manufacturer needs to formulate a detailed line allocation plan to suit customer needs. The detailed production plan is normally formulated upstream from delivery dates.

Queue time between work stations is a critical component for detailed scheduling because it is a major factor determining the production period. In order to shorten the production period, set-up time between work stations should be minimized in addition to shortening pre-production arrangements and processing time. Lot division and parallel line operation may also be considered.

In the case of job order production, increases in order bookings can be accommodated by extending the delivery date. In the case of machine tool manufacturing, a backlog of six months means the production equipment is scheduled for full operation during the coming six month period. A frequent or substantial delivery date extension, however, will alienate customers.

Since a limited number of machines deal with numerous types of processes, operations do not necessarily progress smoothly according to the original production plan. There can be unexpected delays or accelerations. Therefore, field supervisors carefully determine which processes should come first and which processes should follow in accordance with the changing work environment. This function is called "launching." It is helpful for field supervisors to have some basic rules for "launching." There unfortunately are not any fail-safe rule, but the following equation is deemed useful.

$$\text{Priority Index} = \frac{\begin{matrix}\text{Time remaining}\\ \text{to due date}\end{matrix} - \left(\begin{matrix}\text{Remaining}\\ \text{processing time}\end{matrix} + \begin{matrix}\text{Remaining}\\ \text{queue time}\end{matrix}\right)}{\text{Number of operations remaining}}$$

The lower the priority index in the above equation, the higher the priority. Negative figures means that queue time should be shortened.

After the launching, progress should be monitored carefully. Such monitoring is necessary for quick detection of unscheduled delays due to equipment break down and delivery date acceleration to suit customer needs. The use of a computer is recommended for the monitoring if economically viable. The management responsible for launching and progress monitoring highly favours the use of computers if it deals with a large number of orders.

Another point, requiring particular emphasis in scheduling control, is the generation of defects during production. The elimination of defects is a dream for the manufacturer and is destined to remain so in the foreseeable future. At present, defects are unavoidable. This means the input to the production line should be slightly larger than the exact quantity required to satisfy the quantity for delivery. If the input level is too high, there will be waste in terms of excessive production. If the input level is too low, there will be waste in terms of additional miniature lot production for a shorter delivery period. A wise decision is required on the determination of input levels.

9.3.2. Line Production of Automobiles

Like MRP, the formation of work schedules works upstream from delivery dates. First, a schedule for the final assembly process is worked out, followed by schedules for subassembly manufacturing and parts fabrication in that order. Finally, integration takes place among the three schedules.

The final assembly involves a large number of parts and components. Assembly should take place strictly in accordance with instructions which are different on a car-to-car basis. These instructions physically accompany each car body down the line in the forms of signs, stickers, and labels. In order to ensure a smooth assembly operation, the work schedule should allow approximately equal time frames to each work station. This is called work synchronization.

Let us examine how subassembly or component assembly is different from final product assembly. First, the output from subassembly is slightly larger than what is required for final assembly. Surplus components are to accommodate line defects and demand for spare parts.

Second, the time frame for component assembly occasionally varies and does not agree with the time frame for final assembly. Adjustment between the two time frames is made through overtime, three-shift operation, and special-case line mobilization.

Third, numerous parts and components are mostly standardized, which makes it possible for suppliers to mass produce and mass-assemble for delivery to more than one assembly manufacturer.

Last, component assembly tends to take place intermittently and in small lots in order to deliver exactly what is needed and when, although parts for component assembly are mass fabricated and stored for use at short notice. Since the assembly work involved is repetitive in nature, it is comparatively easy to speed up the pre-production arrangements and assembly process.

The planning and control of parts fabrication, component assembly, and product assembly should be implemented in a well-balanced manner. The LOB line formation methodology is often used for this purpose. It presupposes the lead time for each product assembly, component assembly, and part fabrication. The monthly schedule for production volume is worked out for a certain period of time. The process is similar to that for MRP. The comparison between planned schedule and performance figures reveals imbalance, if any, in the production flow. In this case, it is important to grasp the total picture from fabrication to final assembly.

9.4 INVENTORY CONTROL

Inventory control is geared to the reduction and maintenance of standard inventory. Inventory control is of no use if its implementation inflates inventory and total cost. Inventory control should aim at smooth production and minimal inventory realized as a result of inventory reduction at every stage of the production process.

The significance of inventory control exhibits itself when numerous types of materials, parts and products are related to production. Inventory control has been in use for a considerable number of years as an important means of production management together with scheduling control. The original economic model for realizing smooth production at a low inventory level was introduced as far back as the 1910s. In this chapter, two representative methodologies of inventory control and the determination of economical production lot or order quantity are discussed.

The two representative methodologies are the *fixed quantity method* which places an order when inventory dips below a certain prescribed level and the *periodic ordering method* which places an order at regular intervals irrespective of inventory level. The former methodology requires constant monitoring of inventory, which may be extremely time consuming for large inventories. Therefore, the cost reduction from a smaller inventory should more than offset the monitoring cost.

The periodic ordering system appears to be economical when there are a large number of control items. However, the lack of item-to-item inventory monitoring may result in excessive inventory on some items and abnormally low inventory on others, because ordering is not structured to suppress variations in inventory level. This shortfall can be rectified by combining the two methodologies.

For instance, on the basis of a periodic ordering system, items showing abnormally high levels of inventory may be excluded from the ordering list while items showing abnormally low inventory levels may be ordered on an ad hoc basis.

Irrespective of inventory control methodologies, order quantity determines inventory level. Average inventory should be maintained at the 50% level of regular orders. If the order quantity is reduced by 50%, inventory is also reduced by 50%. Optimal order quantity is a key to effective inventory control (see Figure 6-1 in Section 6-3 of Chapter 6).

The lead time from receiving an order to delivery should be considered, particularly in the case of fixed quantity ordering. The question of uncertainty should also be taken into consideration. Inventory control should accommodate changes in lead time and in inventory consumption rate. Counter-measures for such changes include the creation of a safety stock, which can accommodate contingent orders from customers. However, truly effective inventory control should preclude the need for a safety stock.

How is economical ordering quantity determined? Here is a classical model used for that purpose. In this model,

TIC = total annual cost
Q = ordering quantity (production or purchase lot)
C = unit cost
S = ordering cost per order (set up costs or ordering cost for purchasing)
Y = total annual ordering quantity
I = annual inventory cost per unit expressed in percentage.

Annual ordering cost is obtained by multiplying S by the number of purchases for the year which is $\frac{Y}{Q}$. Therefore,

$$\text{annual ordering cost} = \frac{Y}{Q} \times S.$$

The inventory cost is expressed as unit inventory cost per year multiplied by average annual inventory, which is $Q \times \frac{1}{2}$. Therefore,

$$\text{total inventory cost} = \frac{Q}{2} \times C \times I.$$

Assuming there is no cost involved other than the ordering and inventory costs,

$$TIC = \frac{Y}{Q} S + \frac{Q}{2} CI.$$

In order to obtain the most economical volume of order (Q), the righthand side of the above equation is differentiated with reference to Q assuming TIC′ = 0. Then

$$-\frac{Y}{Q^2} \times S + \frac{1}{2} \times CI = 0$$

Then the solution (Q_0) is expressed as,

$$Q_0 = \sqrt{\frac{2YS}{CI}}$$

Q_0 thus obtained is the optimal lot size for ordering. In this case, average inventory is expressed as $\frac{Q_0}{2}$. Orders are issued to minimize cost under given conditions irrespective of the inventory control methodology applied.

9.5 SCHEDULING AND INVENTORY CONTROL FOR SMALLER FIRMS

Since scheduling and inventory control is a basic tool for production management, its implementation should bring about good results in one way or another. Simplified control is recommended for smaller firms from the standpoint of effectiveness. This section deals with MRP, Gantt Chart and ABC analysis for implementation by smaller firms.

9.5.1 MRP for Smaller Firms

MRP was already discussed in Section 9.2 of this chapter. This section delineates the significance of MRP for smaller firms. MRP clearly recognizes the difference in demand between finished products such as automobiles or electrical appliances and parts used to manufacture those finished products. Demand for finished products is beyond the control of the manufacturer because it is generated outside of the corporate framework. In this sense, demand is independent of the manufacturer.

Demand for parts is completely dependent on demand for products. In other words, parts fabrication is characterized by its dependence on demand for finished products. Since smaller firms are mostly suppliers to large manufacturers, they have to be able to produce what is needed and when needed. This type of production drastically reduces inventory. Scheduling control for that purpose is extremely effective for suppliers endeavouring to minimize inventory. MRP is an effective means of reducing inventory and shortening lead time for production and should be used as much as possible.

9.5.2 Gantt Chart

The Gantt Chart was the most important means of scheduling control before World War II. After the war, the birth of operations research attracted greater attention to linear programming (LP). The Gantt Chart was then criticized as being incapable of formulating optimal plans. The application of linear programming should be economical and flexible because working conditions are extremely volatile. It is difficult to use linear programming in this way. However, simplicity and flexibility are inherent to the Gantt Chart and it should be re-evaluated.

PERT has put the Gantt Chart back into the limelight. The PERT network is regarded as a direct derivative of the Gantt Chart. Large projects are controllable by PERT and smaller projects are controllable by Gantt Chart. In both cases, however, proper timing and quantity decisions have to be made in order to produce what is needed when it is needed.

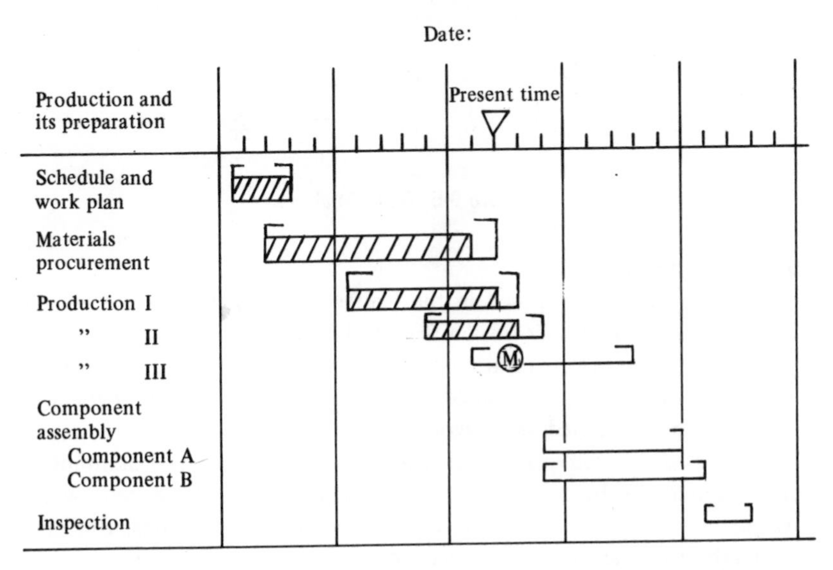

Source: Martin K. Starr, *Operations Management*, Prentice-Hall, 1978 p. 135.

Figure 9-4 A Gantt Planning Chart

A typical Gantt Chart is shown in Figure 9-4. The chart can be applied not only for field works but also pre-production managements. The chart can be more detailed according to actual needs. The beginning and the end point for each activity are indicated by the frame notation. Hatched bars indicate work in progress. The Ⓜ notation indicates a materials shortage. The ∇ notation indicates the present time. Daily up-dating of this chart clarifies progress in all related work categories. Continuous data collection is indispensable for such up-dating.

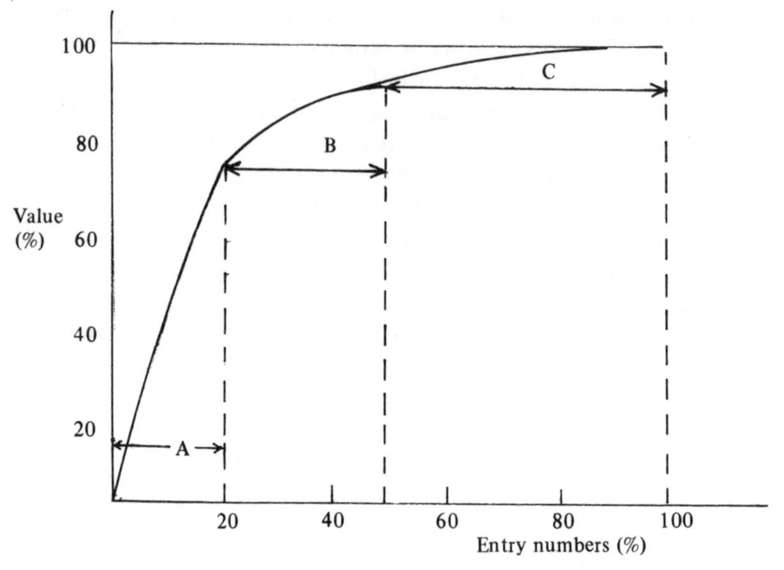

Figure 9-5 ABC Analysis

9.5.3 ABC Analysis

ABC analysis, proposed in the United States, has been successfully implemented by numerous smaller firms in Japan.

First, inventory items are listed top down in the order of their book value. Items in the top portion of the list, accounting for 75% of the total inventory, are classified as category A items and are subject to stringent control based on fixed quantity ordering in most cases. A physical inventory check should also be conducted on these critical items. These items would occupy about 20% of all book entries, with minor variations, from one corporation to the next. Items accounting for 15% of the total inventory and listed below the 75% line are classified as category B items. These items would account for approximately 30% of the total number of entries. The balance, which claims 10% in value and about 50% in terms of entry numbers, are classified as category C items. Less stringent control is enforced on category B items compared with category A, and on category C items compared with category B. Periodic ordering is deemed suitable for category C items. See Figure 9-5 for an illustration of the classification.

Chapter 10
INTEGRATED PRODUCTION MANAGEMENT

Production management should be designed to enhance product competitiveness by way of efficient input-output systems. For that purpose, integrated production management of quality, quantity, time, and cost is necessary. Its implementation should be based on workers' initiative, self-training, and co-operative work participation. This chapter clarifies these points through an explanation of the Toyota production system.

10.1 INTEGRATED PRODUCTION MANAGEMENT AND TOYOTA-STYLE PRODUCTION MANAGEMENT

10.1.1 Significance of Integrated Production Management

As discussed elsewhere in this book, production management should encompass not only quality, work, time, quantity, and cost, but also profit, corporate strategy, and the changing business environment. In order to reap profits, production management should be coordinated with marketing. Corporate strategy should influence the production management methodology. Production management should also accommodate changes in the technical as well as the social environment surrounding the corporation (See Figure 1-2 in Section 1-2 of Chapter 1).

Production management calls for productivity improvement in every aspect of production including pre-production arrangements, product planning and design, and research and development. More important, optimal relations should be established among these control parameters. This is what we call management of systems. Prior to research and development, market surveys, technology assessment, and technology forecasting should be subject to management. Therefore, production management in its wider meaning should cover these parameters as well. (See Figure 1-1, Section 1-1, Chapter 1).

10.1.2 Characteristics of the Toyota Production System

This section reviews a type of production management implemented by those corporations belonging to the Toyota Family consisting of Toyota Motor Co., its subsidiaries, and suppliers (sub-contractors). It is an integrated type of production management. During the decade beginning in 1965, Toyota successfully implemented a revolutionary production management concept involving quality, quantity, and cost. According to this concept, inventory and cost controls should include quality and scheduling controls.

A quality product does not mean much if achieved in exchange for drastically higher production cost. Likewise, complete production management is of little value if its implementation increases production cost. The Toyota concept demands that cost reduction be accompanied by quality improvement. Toyota further maintains that this is achievable through the realization of shorter lead time and smaller inventory.

The Toyota Production System is market-oriented. Production cost needs to be reduced drastically through improvement and innovation in order to beat competition. In order to cope with volatile demand in the market, Toyota has devised a new means of producing a quality car in a short time period following the receipt of a customer's order. Toyota's production management is geared for economical production of limited quantity rather than inexpensive mass-production.

The automative industry can expect frequent model changes because of tough competition. Frequent model changes mean frequent modifications in R & D, product planning, product design, pre-production arrangements, and production lines. In this sense, it is very important to realize time savings throughout the line and to optimize coordination between production phases. Toyota endeavours to shorten the time required for "start-up", the period from product planning to initial production in full scale. They try to eliminate waste, deviation from standard, and strain. Frequent line changes are also subject to rigorous management. This type of production management is related to changes in corporate strategy.

The Toyota Production System has proven its compatibility with new technologies such as robotics and FMS which Toyota began implementing in the 1980s. Toyota's response to worker's increasing levels of education and career consciousness is the creation of new jobs and titles both horizontally and vertically. For instance, assembly workers are trained to perform a variety of jobs related to the assembly line.

Machine operators are trained to perform maintenance. Workers are encouraged to come up with suggestions. This may be called an environment -oriented production management.

Stability and instability alternate. Insistence on stability would tend to make production inflexible in spite of changing demand. Rather than ignoring environmental changes, production management should aim at quickly accommodating them. During a transition period, stability and instability may exist side by side. In addition to the realization of routine production goals, field supervisors are expected to take the initiative in implementing a variety of improvement-oriented changes based on voluntary participation of workers at the shop floor level. This situation is occurring in those corporations enjoying a competitive edges. In such cases, production management may even tolerate the co-existence of stability and instability.

10.2 THE "KAN-BAN" SYSTEM

The dominant characteristic of the Toyota Production System is the "Kan-ban" system. The Japanese word "Kan-ban" has been adopted by a number of Western languages. In substance it denotes production and transport order(s) for repetitive application. "Kan-ban" should contain all the information required for shop level activity, indicated in such a manner that would enable comprehension at a glance. See Figure 10-1 for a typical example of a "Kan-ban".

Job Identification in colour

Production
Order Number ____________

Company
Name ________

Plant
Name ________

Part Number	
Description	

Next Storage
Locations Upstream
& Downstream ____________

Package Type:
Quantity
per pack ______

Job Identification in colour

Figure 10-1 A Typical "Kan-ban"

A pallet of components goes with a "Kan-ban." The number of components on the pallet should always agree with the number specified on the "Kan-ban." In other words, "Kan-ban" checks inventory on a continual basis. The moment a pallet is emptied, its "Kan-ban" turns into a production order to suppliers, and when a pallet has been loaded with components at the suppliers' shipping yard, its "Kan-ban" becomes a shipping order to the trucking company. Functionally, "Kan-ban" in the former application is called "Production Kan-ban" and in the latter application, "Transport Kan-ban."

A "Kan-ban" circulates only among those who are directly involved in one job. The number of "Kan-ban" in circulation is determined on a monthly basis by field managers (foremen and their deputies). Efforts are directed towards reduction in the number of "Kan-ban" in circulation. Fewer "Kan-ban" mean less line inventory. Each "Kan-ban" represents an amount of inventory equivalent to one pallet, and the number of "Kan-ban" indicates the maximum amount of inventory for a certain process. In other words, "Kan-ban" is an effective means of controlling total line inventory volume.

This relation is expressed in the equation,

$$K = \frac{D(T_p + T_w)(1 + \alpha)}{b}$$

where, K = number of "Kan-ban" in circulation
b = capacity of one pallet
D = hourly consumption of parts on pallet
T_p = time required for production or transportation
T_w = idling time for "Kan-ban"
α = capability co-efficient of the workforce, arbitrarily determined by field managers. The maximum capability is defined as $\alpha = 0$.

The term $(1 + \alpha)$ is provided for adjustment in cases when efforts to reduce inventory at the shop level are not sufficient. Field managers should encourage and train workers at the shop floor level in order to minimize the value of α. The value D is determined by demand and is therefore beyond the control of field managers. However, T_p and T_w are subject to constant reduction effort. After reducing the values of α, T_p and T_w, b is also reduced. The ultimate objective is to minimize the value of $K \times b$.

One of the major characteristics of a "Kan-ban" is its reverse flow upstream (see Figure 10-2). ① The volume of parts consumption at the final assembly stage is determined by demand coming through marketing. ② Pallets with 'transport kan-ban' are

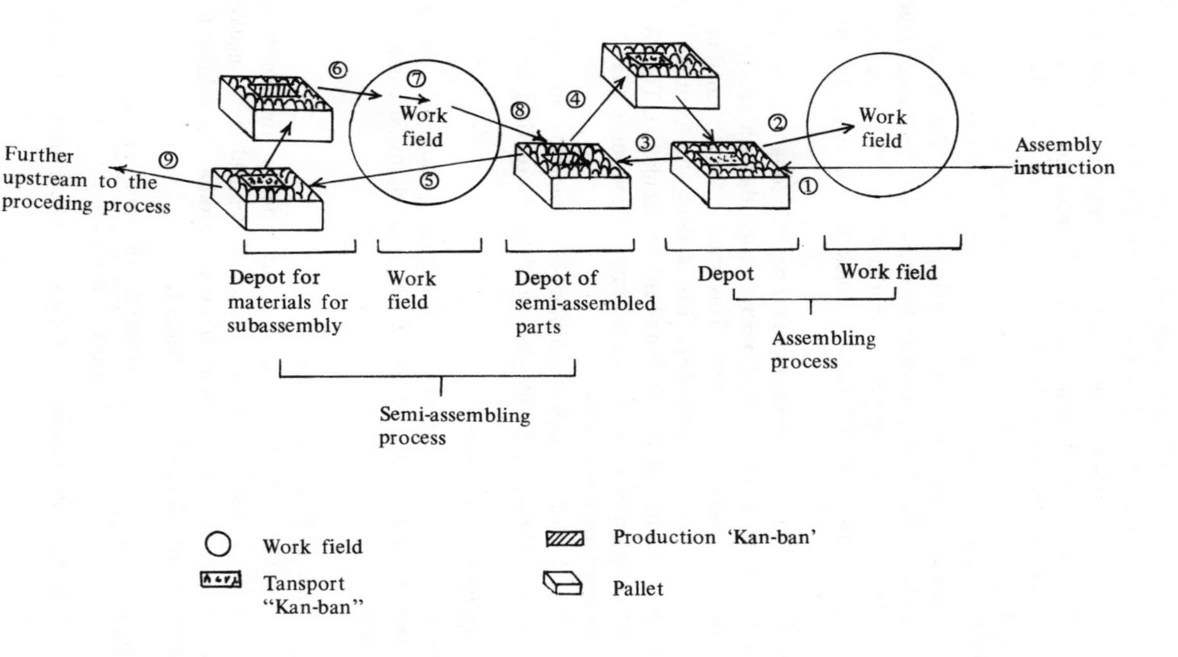

Figure 10-2 Circulation of "Kan-ban"

emptied as a result of assembly work, and ③ the 'kan-ban' on the pallet flows back to the sub-assembly depot to pick up a fresh supply of sub-assemblies in the amount specified on the 'kan-ban' for the final assembly line. ④ The same 'kan-ban' is attached to a fully loaded pallet for transport to the final assembly line. ⑤ The 'production kan-ban' that was originally attached to the loaded pallet is removed from the pallet and transferred up-stream to pick up parts for the sub-assembly line. ⑥, and ⑦ The loaded pallet is emptied for sub-assembly at the work field. ⑧ Sub-assembled parts are loaded on the pallet to which the 'production kan-ban' is attached. ⑨ The 'transport kan-ban' that is removed from the pallet at the parts depot up-stream of the sub-assembly line travels further up-steam to the material yard to pick up materials for parts fabrication.

The Toyota Production System makes it possible for a manufacturing plant to produce what is needed and when needed through an effective deployment of the "Kan-ban" system. This means the elimination of waste in terms of excessive inventory. The system also controls line inventory in terms of the number of "Kan-ban" in circulation. The "Kan-ban" system is also an effective means of information control as "Kan-ban" carries only the necessary information.

The system facilitates implementation of a monthly production schedule while encouraging participation on the part of field workers.

10.3 ELIMINATION OF WASTE

The exclusion of waste is one of the basic philosophies in the Toyota Production System. The waste of labour needs to be eliminated in the first place.

10.3.1 Elimination of Waste of Labour

At Toyota, work standards are used as the criterion for identifying waste of labour. Work standards are a product of demand in the market and so is the daily production volume. When the production volume for the month is set through demand in the market,

$$\text{Daily Production Volume} = \frac{\text{Monthly Production Volume}}{\text{Number of Work Days per Month}}.$$

Cycle time is defined as the number of daily work hours divided by daily production volume,

$$\text{Cycle Time} = \frac{\text{Number of Work}}{\text{Hours per Day}} \div \left(\frac{\text{Monthly Production Volume}}{\text{Number of Work Days per month}}\right).$$

The cycle time concept is used as a basis for work force allocation. Waste of labour can be detected by this process. If all workers observe a certain cycle time calculated by the above equation, the daily production should not require any overtime nor should the day's work be over too early. If the day's work is over before the shift is over, there is a waste of labour somewhere in that work station.

Suppose there is a work station with four workers working eight hours a day. If this work station can complete the day's work two hours before the end of the shift, there is an "idle time" of eight hours (two hours × four persons). This means the work station can operate satisfactorily with three workers instead of four.

Who should leave the work station in this case? Should it be the most competent of the four, the least competent, or the worker with average competence? The standing practice is for the most competent one to leave this work station, enabling him to learn what goes on in other work stations to prepare himself for promotion to the status of foreman.

The person, who leaves the work station, joins the task force before being assigned to a new job. People in the task force help departments that are short of hands or assist stations in improving their work.

The exclusion of waste does not and should not mean exclusion of the weakest. Teamwork at the shop floor level is an extremely important factor. Veteran workers should help and train inexperienced workers on-the-job. When inexperienced workers have acquired sufficient knowledge and experience, veterans are ready to leave the station for further growth. It is not the bullying of the weak.

In order to facilitate the elimination of 'waste of labour,' Toyota implements a flexible work force organization. More specifically, the number of workers per line or work station varies on a day-to-day basis according to the number of "Kan-ban" which functions as work orders for the line or work stations. When the number of "Kan-ban" for the day is not many, the most competent workers of the group form a task force to assist other work stations or to engage in production process improvement, precluding the generation of 'waste of labour.'

The same methodology is applicable to the management of inventory, equipment, quality, information, and transportation. The same "Kan-ban" system is used for information control to achieve the purpose. Here, the "Kan-ban" deletes unnecessary information thereby simplifying management. The application to inventory control will be discussed in a subsequent section. Let us now examine briefly the elimination of 'waste' in equipment, quality, and transportation.

10.3.2 Elimination of Waste in Equipment, Quality, and Transportation

Low cost automation (LCA) is the answer to excluding waste in equipment. Cost efficiency should be sought rather than the hasty introduction of advanced production technologies requiring exorbitant investment. Precautions should be taken to minimize breakdowns as well as time needed for the repair work. Necessary measures should be taken at the time of equipment introduction.

Quality control should prevent excessively high quality. A "Baka-yoke" or defect exclusion device should be installed at each work station for detection and immediate removal of defects before feeding them to the next station upstream. This eliminates waste in the form of further work on defects at the next station.

In transportation, extensive use of conveyors should be avoided in order to minimize the amount of "floating inventory." Deliveries from suppliers should be in the "mixed-loading" format. Frequent deliveries will also reduce total inventory.

10.4 INVENTORY COMPRESSION

The focal concept for the Toyota Production System is inventory compression. "Kan-ban" is an effective means of realizing this concept. Toyota defines inventory as the source of all evils, and there is a lot of truth in this thinking. People always try to dispose of large inventory accumulation at work sites. If there is not enough space to accommodate the inventory between processes, a warehouse becomes necessary. Then one has to employ warehouse attendants. If the warehouse expands, one has to use forklifts with drivers. At night, warehouses must be watched by guards. If the number of employees for warehouses increases, a manager must be assigned. A considerable investment will have been made at this stage, including the construction fee for the warehouse, necessary equipment investment, and personnel expenses plus increases in operational cost. This should be avoided unless additional profit is generated in excess of the costs related to the expanded inventory. Inventory always means additional cost. Invariably, one should take drastic measurement at the assembly line before renting additional warehouse space.

The Toyota Production System focuses its attention on lot inventory caused by line changes. Work in progress, line inventory between work stations, and contingency parts are also subject to rigorous examination. The lot inventory can be reduced by reducing the size of the production lot. But this means more frequent line changes and order issuance. Consequently, the time required for set-up and order processing should be shortened so as not to lower productivity.

According to the Toyota Production System, inventory compression is achieved through the shortening of set-up time. Lot sizes of deliveries from suppliers are also reduced drastically. To achieve this, delivery frequency is increased. Minimization of production lot size by way of shorter set-up time was already discussed in Section 6-3, Chapter 6. Improvements in production techniques make it possible to reduce the time required for set-up. In all extreme case, set-up time has been reduced from 300 minutes to less than ten minutes. Such drastic economies make frequent line changes in small lot production economically viable.

Lot inventory is also reduced through application of the MRP concept (See Section 9-2 of Chapter 9). In component fabrication, just-in-time production of exact quantities of components is crucial in shortening delivery periods and reducing inventory. The Toyota Production System takes full advantage of this concept.

Shortening the time required for assembly and processing also results in a smaller line inventory. It means improvement of the entire production flow. Automation and process integration revolutionized the manufacturing industry. Efforts are now being made wherever possible to combine the two processes into one to reduce the lot size. The final goal is the fabrication of units, one by one as needed, thereby minimizing the time required for the final assembly.

The Toyota Production System calls for drastic reduction in the volume of inventory between work processes. Efforts are being made to load the inventory for any two adjacent stations on one pallet. The system precludes contingency inventory as preparation for breakdowns. One should experience the acute pain of shutting down the entire production line due to a breakdown in one machine. Breakdowns should hurt. The pain should not be eased by the patchwork of contingency inventory. Contingency inventory discourages vigilance and causes "waste". An optimal layout should be obtained during the initial introduction of the equipment, and through rigourous preventive maintenance the frequency of breakdowns should be reduced to zero.

Physical inventory should not exist outside the designated area. This system forces workers to physically restrict inventory to a certain volume without resorting to any theory or calculation. For instance, if one agrees to keep his books in a bookcase and nowhere else, he either disposes of some books or gives up buying new ones when the book case is full.

Inventory reduction should be implemented throughout the manufacturing industry. Field workers should clearly understand the reasons why the inventory should be reduced. After establishing consensus on this major objective, a small group of workers executes its own ideas geared to achieving performance goals. These ideas are refined and strengthened through cooperation among the group members as well as by healthy emulation of other groups.

Reporting meetings are held and teams that demonstrate excellent performance are recognized. Such group activity has been used effectively for inventory reduction. Inventory reduction by the Toyota Production System has revolutionalized work management. The system has succeeded because it employs superb production management methodologies.

10.5 APPLICATION TO SMALLER FIRMS

The Toyota Production System manages people, money, and goods in an integrated manner. The system is extremely market-oriented. The system calls not only for attainment of established goals but also for target modification by the workers themselves. It has proved that good production management should relate to target enhancement as well as daily management routines.

The Toyota Production System, however, is not a panacea. The exclusion of "waste" in extreme cases may preclude the generation of innovative ideas. Consideration should be given to the fact that people differ from machines.

It should be noted also that success of the Toyota Production System hinges on the participation of capable and motivated workers at the shop floor level. Mechanical introduction of the "Kan-ban" system alone does not reduce inventory. An enthusiastic work force centred around capable leaders is the key to success. Reorganization of the work force to ensure constant improvement is the foundation of the system.

The Toyota Production System calls for exclusion of "waste", reduction in production cost, and a supply of quality products to the market at reasonable prices. This concept is in basic agreement with the typical business philosophy of smaller corporations. The problem lies in finding a way to achieve it.

Toyota owes its success to worker training. Therefore, smaller firms desirous of introducing the "Kan-ban" system should begin worker training first. Field workers should be trained to comprehend thoroughly the technical phase of their daily work. The training should proceed according to a prescribed curriculum covering such items as quality control, time control, inventory reduction, cost consciousness, and competition in the market. The ultimate objective of such training is to make workers stand on their own feet and implement work improvements on a voluntary basis.

In parallel with this basic training, short-term projects, of say, six month projects, may be given to workers on such subjects as the shortening of set-up time or the reduction in the rate of defects. These projects should be used to enhance workers' motivation. The workers might compete with each other in coming up with better results according to certain rules and be evaluated in a game-like manner. An interim and a final reporting meeting could be held in which the winners are properly recognized and given prizes.

The success of such a movement depends on the quality and enthusiasm of field leaders. Toyota is successful because they have competent and fully motivated field leaders. Entrepreneurs and managers of smaller firms should follow suit if they wish to be successful. They should do everything possible to foster capable field leaders. It is a time-consuming process requiring a lot of patience. But remember, the Toyota Production System cannot be deployed successfully without able and willing field leaders.

A well trained and motivated work force can identify "waste" and eliminate it. Such a work force knows how to acclimatize the "Kan-ban" system prior to its introduction. Technological improvements during the production phase can be initiated from the grass roots level. In other words, the Toyota Production System is a system that motivates workers to increase productivity and actually participate in such an endeavour. The mechanical details of implementing the system are not so important. "Make haste slowly" is a standing motto for the Toyota Production System.

APPENDIX: SIGNIFICANCE OF TOYOTA PRODUCTION SYSTEM IN MODERN PRODUCTION MANAGEMENT*

1. INTRODUCTION

The Toyota production system is a product of sophisticated strategic concepts, completely independent from conventional expertise. For instance, the drastic trimming of inventory pursued in the Toyota system goes far beyond that conventionally popular concept of "economic production lot size" used as the basis of inventory control models for the past several decades. Conventionally, economical production was attainable only through the reduction of set-up cost. The Toyota production system denies this philosophy for the sake of truly economical production. It is a revolutionary way of thinking. Drastic reduction in set-up time dramatically exemplifies the revolutionary nature of the Toyota system which is designed to change not only production set up but also the entire work environment.

It is important to understand also that the Toyota system is compatible with small-scale production of a large variety of products, a perfect strategic tool with which to tide over a recession. That is the very reason why a large number of manufacturing companies turned to the Toyota system after the oil crisis.

This article is based on the facts, observations and discussions collected and experienced by the author for the past several years at Toyota Jidosha Kogyo K.K. and its affiliates engaged in automobile production in accordance with the Toyota system.

The references include: "Toyota Production System and the 'Kanban' System – Materialization of the Just-in-Time and Respect-for-Human

---

*Reproduced with permission from the IE Review, 113, Vol. 20, No. 1, 1979, published by the Japan Industrial Engineering Association.

System", *International Journal of Production Research,* Vol 15, 1973, Nos. 6, 19, and 7; and *"Toyota Production System* by Taiichi Ohno, (in Japanese) published by Diamond Sha in 1978, and other Toyota intra-company publications.

2. OUTLINE OF THE TOYOTA PRODUCTION SYSTEM

2.1 No strain, no waste, and no deviation from standard

2.1.1 Elimination of Waste

Workers failing to participate aggressively in production are like hangers-on who expect their colleagues to feed them. Surplus workers often become such hangers-on without realizing it. The Toyota system is geared to eliminate surplus workers from the production line for that very reason. To begin with, standard work is defined rigorously which workers must observe. Workers are instructed to leave their work stations to report in the designated area nearby the moment they complete such standard work. In this manner, one can tell clearly how much idle time each worker has during the day. Those work stations generating idle time constantly are instructed to let the best workers go to form a special task force. Members of such a task force, well trained in all the facets of production skills, make suggestions, trouble shoot, and give a helping hand to work stations upon request.

After the elimination of surplus workers, the members of a work station assist each other more closely, creating a group spirit. The strong help the weak. Needless to say, it is very important at this stage to clearly define the number of workers required to accomplish the given amount of work. Surplus workers, generated as a result of this process, join the task force to render ad hoc assistance to work stations and to study the ways and means of improving the existing work steps when no assistance is required at work stations.

Field supervisors should be capable of mobilizing workers, while encouraging them to come up with suggestions. Workers in the task force are candidates for field supervisors, rather than less competent surplus workers. Competent persons can enhance their capabilities through the rendering of assistance to different work stations. In addition to the acquisition of production skills and improvement ideas, these selected people would learn the art of grasping the entire production line as a living organism.

2.1.2 Inventory Compression

Inventory compression is one of the key elements to the Toyota production system. A large inventory in the field is classified as a tangible proof of strain, waste and deviation from standard. Accordingly, inventory compression or reduction should bear tangible fruit. It is possible to set up a clear cut goal specifying location and quantity. Everybody understands easily what the fulfilment of such a goal means. It is a persuasive, convincing and challenging process. Challenging because the further one reduces inventory, the more difficult it becomes to go a small step further. There are five ways of inventory compression as specified below.

1) **Compression of Buffer Inventory**

Inventories are often accumulated at the interface of work stations having different process capacities. Such inventories should be eliminated first of all.

Breakdowns of machines may also generate internal buffer inventory. For instance, if a machine breaks down, inventory is generated at the end of the preceding work station. If the same machine breaks down often, production should be speeded up while the machine is working in order to keep downstream stations running during the break down – another cause of buffer inventory. If the machine can be fixed in a short period, such inventory may not be necessary. In order to eliminate buffer inventory a careful selection of production equipment should be made at the time of initial capital investment. Preventive maintenance should be implemented rigorously in order to avoid major breakdowns. Operators in the field should be well trained to handle minor breakdowns in order to minimize the frequency and duration of down time. These measures, when implemented as a package, would drastically reduce buffer inventory.

2) **Compression of lead-time inventory**

Untimely or prolonged pre-production arrangements, components fabrication, and transportation cause unnecessary inventory. Shroter lead time would certainly reduce inventories of materials, parts, and components waiting processing, fabrication, and assembly work to begin. The shortening in process time reduces the inventory of half-finished products. Quick turn or quick return of the machine from one process to another is one of many efforts to reduce idling time in processing. Shortening the time required for material handling and transportation also contributes to the reduction of inventory for which reduction of lot size is a pre-requisite.

3) **Compression of lot inventory**

As discussed at the beginning of this appendix, the shortening of set-up time made small lot production economically viable. Since the standard inventory level is $\frac{1}{2}$ of the production lot size, one can reduce inventory eight fold by reducing the lot size four fold (See Figure A-1). No wonder the Toyota system emphasizes the necessity of minimizing set-up time.

Lot size was reduced for parts delivery as well. Frequent deliveries

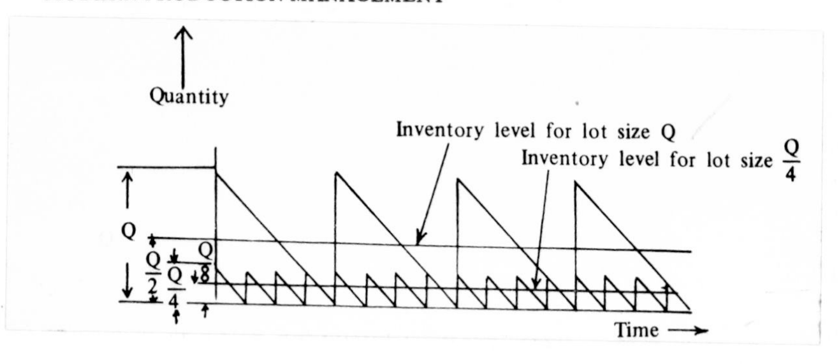

Figure A-1 Relationship between Inventory and Lot Size

from component fabricating factories to assembling factories, using smaller trucks capable of transporting different types of parts in one haul, appreciably reduced parts inventory at the assembly line.

4) Compression of inventory space

The location and size of inventory space should be clearly specified for strict observance. Production inventory is visible. Therefore its reduction is obvious to anybody. According to the Toyota production system, necessary inventory space is calculated for each item (part and component) and clearly marked three-dimensionally. Therefore, excess inventory is discernible at a glance.

5) Use of "Kan-ban" or written signs

"Kan-ban" plays an important role in inventory reduction under the Toyota system. "Kan-ban", extensively used for inventory reduction, refers to a work instruction sheet or job order in a transparent plastic holder which accompanies the pallet holding parts or materials. This "Kan-ban" goes wherever the pallet goes. The number of "Kan-ban" issued for each part is pre-determined on a monthly basis by field supervisors. The total number of "Kan-ban" in circulation determines the size of parts inventory or the number of un-assembled parts wherever they may be. The number of "Kan-ban" in circulation is gradually reduced as workers acquire experience, reducing parts inventory. It is critical to determine the optimal number of "Kan-ban" in circulation from time to time. ("Kan-ban" does not have to come in a document format. Coloured golf balls are used in certain instances.)

2.1.3 Exclusion of Strain, Waste, and Deviation from Equipment Standards

The Toyota production system sheds light on the mechanism of strain waste, deviation from standards to the equipment which generate unnecessary inventory. It also urges reduction in such inventory in order to optimize equipment utilization.

A thorough cost benefit analysis should be conducted prior to the introduction of new equipment. The introduction of additonal equipment does not necessarily mean enhanced mechanization if the existing equipment is not fully utilized. In other words, additional investment of fixed assets becomes meaningless without elimination of waste on the equipment in use. In this sense, it is recommendable to choose trouble-free equipment at the time of introduction.

Equipment should aim at low-cost automation. It will not be an unbearable financial burden if in-house resources are utilized effectively. An automatic shutdown mechanism should be built to the production line for immediate detection of defects. In the face of rising labour cost, the number of machines per operator should increase.

Automated production lines do not require "operators" per se. Workers supervise or manage the equipment which operates by itself. Worker intervention is required only when the line automatically stops to indicate defective production.

Production lines can be designed to accommodate particular changes in equipment utilization without physical equipment relocation. In this case, the equipment utilization rate is easily determined through the identification of idle equipment without resorting to complex computation procedures.

Preventive maintenance can never be emphasized too much. Such maintenance should be implemented by field workers, if at all possible. As already discussed, set-up time should be shortened in order to reduce lot size and inventory. A higher equipment utilization rate is achievable in this way. Appropriate measures, including personnel allocation, should be provided in order to minimize repair time in the case of equipment break down. Poor equipment management means waste and unnecessary inventory. That is why the introduction and management of equipment are subject to rigorous scrutiny and evaluation at Toyota.

2.1.4 Strain, Waste and Deviation from Standard Quality

The Toyota production system does not call for excessively high quality. From the designing stage on, Toyota products are made to satisfy certain performance and safety requirements, and no more. Defects are immediately removed from the production line. An automatic shutdown mechanism is built into the production line for this very reason. Each defect is repeatedly analysed until the real cause has been identified.

2.1.5 Strain, Waste and Deviation from Standard Information

Unnecessary information should not be given to work stations. Sufficient but minimum amount of information is given depending on needs. Production workers do not have to familiarize themselves with monthly production schedules. They just observe the instructions given by "Kan-ban." They are not authorized to generate new instructions. In this manner, one can avoid confusion and realize efficiency.

2.1.6 Strain, Waste, Deviation from Standards in Production

The Toyota production system eliminates strain, waste, and deviation from standards in inventory, equipment, quality, and information primarily through inventory compression. In order to cope with frequent model changes in compliance with diversified market needs, Toyota presently utilizes another means of waste elimination, the shortening of recovery time for normalization after line changes. Other things being equal, the shortening of lead time and quicker optimization of the production line mean substantial reduction in the number of work steps. This new clout is an aim of the Toyota system.

2.1.7 Cost Reduction

The ultimate goal of the Toyota system is cost reduction. The exclusion of strain, waste, and deviation from standard is a means of achieving this goal. A note-worthy phenomenon in addition to the aforementioned six points is Toyota's debt-free business management. A number of corporations belonging to the Toyota family continued to pay back their debts, even during the period immediately after the oil crisis, to realize debt-free business management. Interest payment is considered to be a type of strain, waste, and deviation from standard. Investments are subject to rigorous evaluation based on return.

2.2 "Kan-ban", its Definition and Functions

2.2.1 Definition

"Kan-ban" is one of the key tools for the implementation of the Toyota production system. It is a work order sheet or tag subject to repetitive circulation in the field. Unlike conventional work orders, "Kan-ban" always accompanies parts or materials thereby facilitating inventory control on the spot. The number of "Kan-ban" in circulation is strictly controlled according to the monthly production schedule, effectively controlling the quantity of unassembled parts and components. A sheet of "Kan-ban" normally corresponds to a full case or a pallet load of parts or components.

"Kan-ban" is issued by the rear end of the production line, which is one of the innovative ideas of the Toyota production system. For instance, the assembly line issues "Kan-ban" to the parts division and suppliers. Therefore, production does not start until demand at the rear end has been specified at the front end of the production line. Unlike conventional production systems where the rear end tries to consume whatever is supplied by the front end, excessive parts supply to the rear is an impossibility in the Toyota system.

The number of "Kan-ban" in circulation is trimmed down to a bare minimum for strict inventory control, including parts by the side of the assembly and those in transportation. The reduction of inventory, however, should be achieved without adversely affecting the total production cost. This is made possible through the utilization of innovative technologies. The fewer the number of "Kan-ban" in circulation, the greater the cost reduction in terms of inventory control.

The "Kan-ban" system facilitates modifications in monthly production schedules at short notice. Estimated production quantity per type and model often requires minor modifications depending on order bookings by representatives and dealers. If small lot production is possible for all parts and components, optimum inventory adjustment is made by merely increasing or decreasing the number of "Kan-ban" in circulation for each part. The "Kan-ban" system makes it possible to maintain the bare minimum inventory regardless of total, as well as per model or per type production volume. A smoothing out of work steps after line changes is indispensable to the effective implementation of the "Kan-ban" system.

2.2.2 Function

The function of "Kan-ban" may be summarized in the following six points.

1) "Kan-ban" stimulates initiative on the part of field workers. For instance, it is an effective means of delegating authority to foremen. Foremen, with the authority of issuing "Kan-ban," in turn, can promote group participation by discussing "Kan-ban" issues and recalls with their workers. Foremen can endeavour to reduce the number of "Kan-ban" through training and work improvement. Foremen and assistant foremen are expected to play a catalytic role in promoting work improvement.
2) "Kan-ban" is a means of information control. It sorts necessary information from unnecessary information, thereby achieving maximum results with minimum information.
3) "Kan-ban" controls inventory. Direct inventory control is possible in the field inasmuch as "Kan-ban" always accompanies actual parts or materials. The total inventory is controlled in terms of the number of "Kan-ban" in circulation.
4) "Kan-ban" enhances the sense of belonging among workers. A visible work performance goal is set up for a work station, and workers

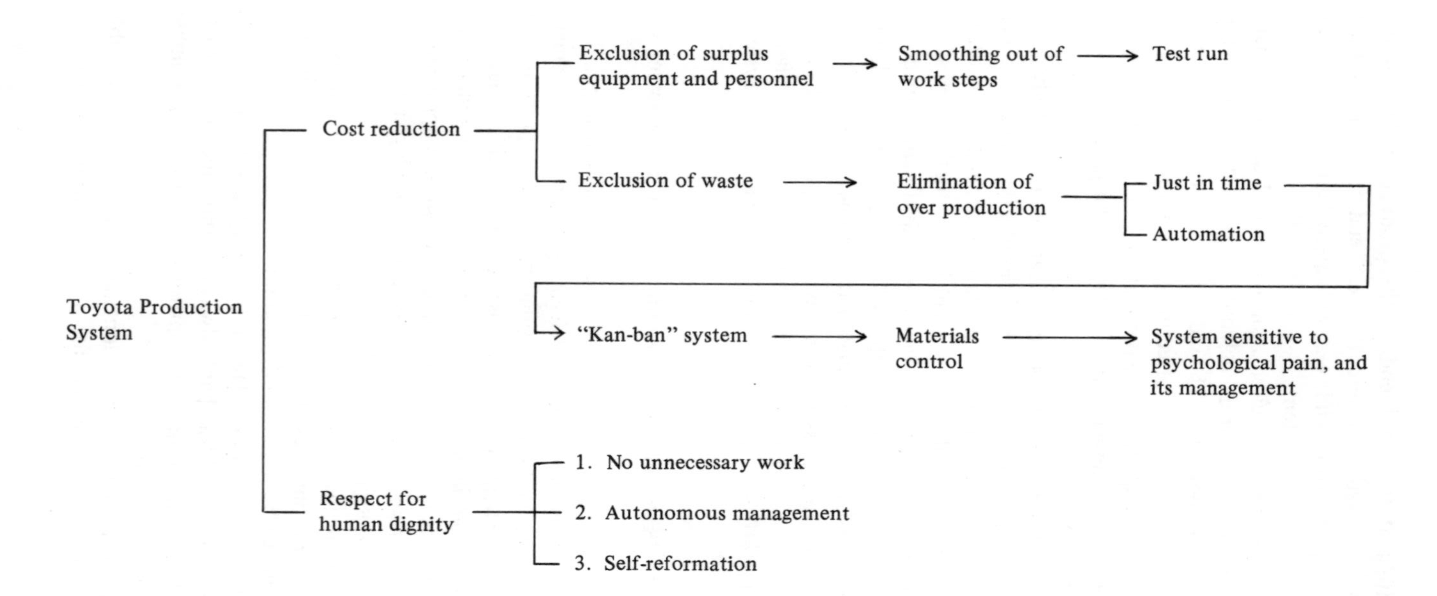

Figure A-2 Structure of the Toyota Production System

Note: The above chart has been compiled based on the information in Toyota's training manual, Toyota's report to the 4th International IE Symposium, and the verbal remarks of Toyota people during their discussions with the author.

belonging to that work station exert their concerted efforts to reach the goal by innovative means. This type of group motivation assures a successful implementation of the Toyota production system.

5) "Kan-ban" simplifies work management mechanisms through information and inventory control, rejuvenating corporate organization.
6) Information and inventory control also enables visual work management in the field. Workers can visually confirm inventory from time to time by observing the number of parts pallets. This stimulates suggestions for further inventory reduction.

2.3 Structure of the Toyota System

Figure A-2, quoted from the report submitted by Toyota to the International IE Symposium, shows the structure of the Toyota production system. This structure, together with the outline described so far in this appendix, is discussed and evaluated in the following section. In the last section, titled "Conclusion," the contribution towards production management is discussed.

3. DISCUSSION AND EVALUATION

3.1 Discussion

The Toyota production system consists of production and management aspects. The production aspect comprises the following:

1) The so-called supermarket type demand-pull format is used. Supermarkets replenish their shelves after the merchandise has been sold and then only to the extent of the volume sold. Toyota transplanted this idea into car making.
2) Toyota implements economical small lot multiple production, which eliminates unnecessary inventory. This philosophy is applicable throughout Toyota's production line, from parts fabrication to trim assembly, including supplies from suppliers. Smaller production lots have multiple effects in terms of inventory reduction (See Fig. A-1).
3) Small-lot production calls for small-lot transport. Delivery trucks carry a variety of parts in small quantities in one haul. As a result, the total physical volume per haul tends to decrease whereas the number of hauls per day increases.
4) Quality checking is automated. Defects are automatically identified and removed from the production line. At the same time, the machine shutdowns automatically to notify defects to the workers. In this way, one can avoid labour waste added to defects if they were not detected until the end of the line.
5) Education is another important feature. The exclusion of waste is

not possible without the participation of every worker in the field. A worker must be sufficiently motivated so he will exert concerted effort at his own initiative under the guidance of his foreman. And motivation is a product of education which sometimes appears to be too time-consuming. For any organizational change, one must go slow and steady.

6) The Toyota system maintains a rather conservative stance regarding automation or mechanization of the production line. A comprehensive standardization of work procedures and steps is required prior to automation. Human labour is substituted first with a new piece of equipment operated by workers. This equipment will not be automated until its operators have been thoroughly acquainted with it. Hasty action may cause unexpected waste.

The management aspect of the system comprises the following:

1) The introduction of the "Kan-ban" system has drastically simplified production management in the field. Field workers have been liberated from the pressure of mammoth corporate organization. By way of a clear-cut production management, the Toyota system enables workers to control the quantity, quality, and cost of products in an integrated manner using only one parameter – inventory control, an important characteristic of the Toyota production system.

2) The management cycle is shortened through the introduction of the "Kan-ban" system, "Kan-ban" being synonymous to demand-pull production and the spirit of trouble-sharing on the part of workers. A huge production plant stays alert down to every worker. In return, certain authority is delegated to workers so that they can cope with problems in the field at their own initiative. A thriving manufacturing plant cannot exist without competent workers.

3) Thorough implementation of visual control is another unique feature of the Toyota system. It is structured in such a way that any anomaly in the system is easily detectable by human eye sight without the help of apparatuses or computer printouts. A red lamp in case of defects, an exceptionally tall heap of pallets, or a flickering lamp tells one there is no parts supply from the work station upstream – these visual signs are built into the system to ensure thorough implementation.

4) Last but not least, the author deems it necessary to discuss autonomous management. Within the Toyota corporate family, there usually is an extensive delegation of authority to field supervisors and foremen. These leaders in the field are authorized to decide on the number of "Kan-ban" in circulation, daily work routines

including overtime, and programmes for improvement suggestions. The best leader in the field is the one who is acquainted with the field work. This is the very philosophy adopted by the Toyota production system. The plant manager and his staff are to give expert advice to the field leader so that he and his workers can make their work environment more modernistic. Toyota has established a unique modus operandi for plant management.

3.2. Evaluation (I)

Let us enumerate the meritorious features of the Toyota production system in order to find out why this system has become famous.

3.2.1

First of all, the Toyota production system is versed in mobilizing workers in the field.

Proper achievement goals should be established to motivate the workers. Those goals should be pragmatic ones based on the consensus of the workers involved. They have to be persuasive and challenging. Although the focal point of the system is inventory compression, this central theme can be implemented in a variety of different ways. Nothing is more effective than a well-chosen target when it comes to the initiation of total involvement by everyone. The target is particularly effective when it is based on total consensus.

Throughout the selection and implementation stages of such a target, leaders of the work force play an important role. According to the material the author obtained recently in Shanghai, China, the linchpin of the successful mass movement at the Dacing Oil Field was a devoted leader who was a showcase to all group leaders in the field. As a result, a farmland factory complex housing some 500,000 people was created out of vacant grassy fields. Likewise, the Toyota production system owes its success to those devoted group leaders who put in a lot of time and energy in the field. The mechanism of people mobilization is the same whether it is in Japan or in China.

The Toyota production system emphasizes team work. Performance targets are reached as a result of mutual cooperation based on the sense of belonging. Small group activities such as quality circles are an effective means of creating a sense of belonging on the part of workers vis-a-vis the company they work for. While deploying a variety of activities designed to reduce inventory to a bare minimum, workers come up with wild ideas which are utterly foreign to conventional systems. Many such ideas were turned into reality achieving inventory reduction and reduction in total cost. The Toyota system substantiates the importance and effectiveness of complete alienation from the conventional way of thinking.

3.2.2

The Toyota system is a means of nurturing people. The system has vitalized work stations through the nurturing of powerful supervisors and foremen. Healthy field leaders grew out of rigorous organizational restructuring. Those capable leaders were fully motivated to educate workers to follow in their steps. On the other hand, workers having value gaps, ill health, and weak minds became dropouts. (This will be discussed later in this appendix).

3.2.3

The Toyota production system controls quantity, quality and cost in an integrated manner with emphasis on the autonomy of field workers. Such production management is a means of making the best use of energy input. The control of one of the three parameters alone does not bring the point home. It has to be an integrated management to control all three parameters simultaneously. Furthermore, the management does not belong to managers alone. It belongs to autonomous organizations of field workers. Based on this philosphy, the Toyota system entrusts field leaders to implement production management with the voluntary help of their workers.

Cost reduction for a work station should not be carried out at the sacrifice of other work stations. Defects should not be passed onto the next station downstream. Rigorous cost benefit analysis is required prior to the introduction of new equipment. These considerations are derived from Toyota's corporate philosophy of assessing long-run efficiency. It is a systematic strategy deployment.

3.2.4

The system demands a certain management format. A simple management mechanism, visual management and voluntary participation by workers are among the ingredients of this format. Waste should be excluded at the source, a concept foreign to the conventional management.

3.3 Evaluation (II)

Despite the merits mentioned in the preceding section, the author sees certain shortcomings in the Toyota production system.

3.3.1

It appears that the Toyota system urges endless cost reduction or complete elimination of inventory. In this context, the Toyota system maintains a daunting and optimistic philosophy. However, in the real world, particularly when the implementation of the system is programmed within a certain time frame, this philosophy is subject to certain limitations. "Too much doing is synonymous with too little doing" as we say it in Japan. Inventory compression as a means of cost reduction does not necessarily provide unlimited opportunities. However, the Toyota system apparently presupposes unlimited opportunities and demands unlimited devotion to grasp such opportunities.

Dissidents are ostracized. This is understandable because the essence of the Toyota system lies in the mobilization of people in the field towards the realization of certain goals. In other words, the system is a well-concocted slogan for rallies.

A well-programmed implementation is the key to success for such a slogan. Hasty implementation without due attention to social and technological environments would invite many undesirable side effects rather than successes. Such side effects would include:

1) The exclusion of waste may be interpreted as the suppression of wild ideas.
2) Inventory compression through the exclusion of strain, waste, and deviation from standard may cause excessive mental strain on the part of field managers. Apparent reduction in physical inventory may mean accumulation of mental strain on the part of workers.
3) The removal of surplus work force may give a sense of instability among field workers, and eventually, a loss of enthusiasm towards work.
4) Spendthrift slashing of inventory does not always mean total cost reduction. The standardization of work steps and procedures may mean inefficiency in extreme cases.

The Toyota system is not onmipotent. It should be implemented cautiously, only after a thorough comprehension of the work environment subjected to the system. Also the implementation should be flexible enough to accommodate compromise between the system and the existing work environment.

3.3.2

The respect for humans advocated by the Toyota system needs refinement. Other than the elimination of unnecessary work, the delegation of authority to field workers, and the promotion of self-enlightenment, there are certain elements the Toyota system should absorb so each field worker with a sound mind and body can exert creative effort for a better life and work environment.

3.3.3

In terms of self-management, management authority is delegated extensively to supervisors and formen, but not to line workers. If the Toyota system aims at self-management in its literal sense, the present status of achievement is by no means satisfactory. Line workers should also be involved directly in self-management.

3.3.4

The Toyota production system creates a peculiar organizational environment. Those who agree with the system become strong individuals, but those who disagree are always in danger of expulsion. The more effective the system, the more conspicuous is this side effect. However, a mere exclusion of dissidents does not provide a real solution to the problem.

3.3.5

"Birds of a feather flocking together" represent formidable power and superb efficiency under certain conditions. But under a completely different set of conditions, they are lost. Lost, because they all think and behave the same way and do not know how to adjust themselves to the new environment. On the other hand, a flock of different birds can accommodate environmental changes although it may not be able to exert a formidable influence under uniform conditions. In this context, companies employing the Toyota system may have a limitation.

3.3.6

Careless introduction of the Toyota production system should be avoided. For instance, adoption of the system by a large manufacturing company inevitably involves and affects its suppliers. A hasty business decision, without due consideration for the unique human relationships under the system, may invite unexpected and undesirable repercussions from suppliers.

3.3.7

There is no scientific evidence supporting the viability of the complete elimination of inventory which is the ultimate goal for the Toyota production system. It is ironic that the further one advances in inventory reduction, the further away this ultimate goal goes. The smaller is the inventory, the better the production situation. However, it is important to establish scientifically optimal inventory levels depending on the time, place, and type of production system. Complete elimination of inventory may be a slogan with which to motivate workers, but it is hardly a theme with scientifc reasoning.

4. CONCLUSION – CONTRIBUTION TOWARDS MODERN PRODUCTION MANAGEMENT

The productive contribution of the Toyota system towards modern production management far outweighs its shortcomings discussed in the previous section. First, the Toyota system bears a strategic significance. Those corporations, introducing flexible manufacturing using robotics, can certainly strengthen their strategic stance during recession through the adoption of the Toyota production system. Second, production management under the Toyota system does not merely mean the adjustment between given standards and performance. Instead, the system urges the alteration of existing standards. It demonstrates that management and innovation exist side by side. This is a significant breakthrough in the nature of production management. Third, the Toyota system adds a fresh page to the bible of production management by introducing integrated one parameter control of quality, quantity, and cost. The system motivates and mobilizes workers in the field so they contribute voluntarily towards the betterment of technology and human relations in terms of production efficiency. Production management encompasses both technological and human elements. The Toyota system suggests an entirely new method of analyzing these two elements simultaneously under one scheme. The test of the management design is in the realization of pragmatic production goals and not in the refinement of the management methodology itself. In this sense, the Toyota system is a monument in the history of production management. Particularly, the idea of self-management in the field through the delegation of authority is a step towards further evolution of production management.